Boyce !
TO MY ~...

Women Elders' Life Stories of the Omaha Tribe

UNIVERSITY OF NEBRASKA PRESS | LINCOLN AND LONDON

Women Elders' Life Stories of the Omaha Tribe

Macy, Nebraska, 2004–2005 | Wynne L. Summers

© 2009
by the
Board of Regents
of the
University of Nebraska
All rights reserved
Manufactured in the
United States of America
⊚
Library of Congress
Cataloging-in-Publication Data

Summers, Wynne L.
Women elders' life stories of the
Omaha Tribe: Macy, Nebraska,
2004–2005 / Wynne L. Summers.
p. cm.
Includes bibliographical references
and index.
ISBN 978-0-8032-2536-7
(cloth: alk. paper)
1. Omaha women—Nebraska—Macy—
Biography. 2. Older women—Nebraska—
Macy—Biography. 3. Omaha Indians—Nebraska—Macy—Biography. 4. Indian leader-
ship—Nebraska—Macy. 5. Baxter, Eleanor.
6. Saunsoci, Alice. 7. Háwate. 8. Omaha Indians
—Nebraska—Macy—Social life and customs.
9. Macy (Neb.)—Biography. 10. Oral history—
Nebraska—Macy. I. Title.
E99.O4S86 2009
978.2'004975253—dc22
2009029722

Set in Adobe Garamond
and Futura by Kim Essman.
Designed by R. W. Boeche.

Lines between worlds say much about who we are
Who we are going to be
Our lives in between
White and Indian
Indian and white
Cultures drawn and interwoven between worlds
shadow lands
Borderlands
Of life
But I am caught in between
Living in both
Breathing in both
Working in both
Does that tell you
Who I am?
Stories spoke the first word and brought me
     from the edges of two places
So carefully drawn
Etched in stone
In tobacco
In smoke.
I am the woman in the story
And the story is me
An Omaha woman
A proud woman
Weaver of dreams
Woman of means
Storyteller.

Contents

Illustrations

Following p. 30

Map

Preface

Macy, Nebraska, is the location of the headquarters for the Omaha tribe.[1] When I started my research in Macy in the spring of 2004, it was with an intent other than talking with women about their life stories. I originally wanted to research Omaha-language place names and stories associated with them. Since my graduate school efforts at the University of Nebraska–Lincoln encompassed history, anthropology, and English, I felt that researching place names covered all three in a relevant manner. I additionally had the support of my Omaha language professor, Dr. Mark Awakuni-Swetland, anthropologist, researcher, and scholar.[2] Near the end of the final semester of the two-year program, I asked Mark to suggest a topic that would fulfill my obligation for the doctorate and at the same time give something back to the Omaha community. I felt they had given me much in terms of sharing their language.

The colonial conquest of Native languages by whites remains

a sensitive issue of which I was acutely aware. Creek Native Craig Womack talked about a disassociation from landscape through European colonization, disruption, and removal from home places and land in his book *Red on Red*. This disassociation is also evident in the recontextualizing of Native languages through the cultural implications of white colonization. What allowed reconnections, Womack said in *Red on Red*, was storytelling and learning and speaking Native language. While language is key in making this reconnection, it is a language owned by Native communities and not by whites. In 1930, Creek writer Alexander Posey established a language distinctly "Creek" that he called "este charte," or what Womack rephoneticized *stijaati*. It is a form of Creek-English that incorporates a number of themes reflecting what it means to be Creek though the eyes of Natives who observed the "goings on" of the day and time, then commented on them with humor and insight. The voice of Posey illustrated the importance of the Creek voice in interpreting events. In Posey's narratives, there was an absence of a white colonial voice interpreting Indians. Womack's central point in *Red on Red* was that Native Americans themselves should be not only writing literature but commenting critically on their own works, rather than leaving colonial-rendered English departments to interpret them through critical theory and textual implications. With this much emphasis on Native peoples owning Native language, it was no surprise that our language class had a specified awareness of these cultural implications.

Kimberly Blaeser's exploration of "writing in the oral tradition" examined mixed-blood Anishinaabe poet and critic Gerald Vizenor's work with regard to a sensitivity of voices.

In the introduction to her book *Gerald Vizenor: Writing in the Oral Tradition* she wrote that Vizenor sought to liberate the written word from the colonizing constraints of the English language. She noted that Vizenor has argued that the Indian will survive or "vanish" through the merits of language: survive through tribal oral tradition or be made to vanish through popular, scientific, literary, and political rhetoric. He did, in fact, encourage deconstructing the term "Indian" if Native people are to survive. He wishes to liberate "Indianness" from the constraints of a history that continues to insist on regarding them in the historical context of "stasis and tragedy" (39). Survival, according to Vizenor, is determined by stories that become "a corrective to the popular romantic stories about Indian people." He sees his literary role as that of illuminating "both the sham of contemporary 'Indianness' and the power of vision and dream to restore tribal values" (40).

To counter such static interpretations and move beyond any constrained academic discourses surrounding the production of a formal dissertation, I recognized the need to meet with tribal council members in Macy to obtain their permission and support prior to any interviews and to determine the course of my research on place names and the stories connected to them.[3] In the fall of 2004, I met with tribal secretary Eleanor Baxter at the tribal council building in Macy. Located across from the Umóⁿhoⁿ Nation Public School, it is a round brick building with the door facing east. As I walked inside I was impressed with the circular design, which gave the building a sense of the elements of wood and brick working together. The various clan names and symbols were painted on poles arranged in a circle (ten clans were represented). To the west was the tribal council chamber, where many of the meetings took place.

The council building was a place of constant activity. People came and went from the multiple doors facing the center of the building, where chairs and sofas were often filled with people attending to issues or concerns or waiting to see council members. Eventually, the receptionist told me to go back to where Eleanor's office was located, in what I thought was the "inner sanctum" of tribal politics. I went down a hallway, then into a larger area where more offices were located: the chairperson's' and other members of the tribal council.

I entered Eleanor's office. I found a woman very similar to the image I had formed of her based on prior phone conversations. Eleanor was a beautiful woman, round-cheeked and smiling, with reddish black hair and bold eyes that reflected intuition and intelligence. She seemed at first meeting to be a person who called things as she saw them without mincing words. Formidable, but not in a negative way. Assertive. We shared some Omaha words. "Eóⁿ níⁿ a?" she asked me, which means "How are you?" Eleanor taught me other words I had not heard before, and we laughed at my novice efforts, then talked about the importance of keeping and maintaining the Omaha language for cultural survival. In accordance with Omaha tradition and custom, I had brought cookies and coffee to share. In return, Eleanor gave me a gift, a bluish green metal lizard with a candle in the middle of its body. I said "Pézhitu," which means a kind of green-blue. She shook her head and said, "No, *tú*," meaning "blue." In the middle of our conversation, she stood up and said, "Come with me."

I followed her back out into the circle of council offices, then into another meeting room. On the wall was a large white calendar board. Dates were etched with black markers for upcoming meetings and events. Gathered around a circular table were what I assumed to be several council members. Eleanor looked at a man sitting near me and said, "Chairman Grant. This woman has traveled all the way from Lincoln to meet with us about a project she would like to do." Chairman Grant nodded and pointed to a chair. I took a seat next to him and thanked him for his time. As we talked, I became less uncomfortable and outlined my project proposal. He was not only willing to help me, but receptive to the idea of studying place names in and around Macy and the stories that might be affiliated with those names. I explained that the written document of the project would be given to the Omaha tribe along with copies of interview tapes. The tapes of people interviewed for the project would also be given to the interviewees, if they so desired, and would also go to the archives at the Umóⁿhoⁿ Nation Public School and to the Nebraska Indian Community College.[4] Toward the end of our meeting, he asked for my phone number at work so he could contact me about a future meeting with the rest of the council members to review the project. I told him the university prefix, 472, then finished with the last four digits, 1880. He grinned and said, "Was that a treaty year? You have to learn to joke with us."

This was the beginning of a multitude of meetings with Eleanor, Chairman Grant, and other council members. I prepared more letters to outline my plan and always brought something with me to show my appreciation for their time—cookies, coffee, fruit. Often I brought "friendship bread." This was much preferred over anything else so I frequently made enough loaves to pass around. Toward the end of October, shortly before tribal elections, Chairman Grant gave me approval for the project and signed an appropriate form noting this approval.[5] I was ready to proceed.

Looking back on this hesitant but encouraging beginning, I am reminded of Betty Louise Bell's exploration of family stories in *Faces in the Moon*. The main character, Lucie, an educated "off-rez" Indian, returned home to hear stories from her mother and aunt. "I was raised on the voices of women," Lucie began. "I listen. I grew tired of living in the past and craved to find my stories in narratives of direction and purpose. I lived in the time of choice, where a person has only to believe to make it true" (4–5). Like Bell's character Lucie, I craved stories with "purpose and direction." I outlined what I needed to know and set out to do it, beginning with visits to the senior center in Macy. Chairman Grant had earlier introduced me to the woman who managed the center, Cindy. My routine was to find Cindy, who then took me to where rows of tables were set up for lunches or dinners. She introduced me to whoever was there. One time, it was a woman whose name I do not remember but whose story I do. It was a life story. She talked about her early childhood and the recent loss of her son. She got out a picture of this son as a baby and again talked about her loss and her life of children, of living in Macy, and of leaving and returning. My recorder remained in the bag, the tape silent as she talked. I was after place names, not life stories. But her story haunted me and I remembered it long after I left the center.

On another occasion, I visited with tribal elder Naomi Gilpin on Chairman Grant's recommendation. She lived in a green house south of the council building and south of the C-Store, a small store where gas can be purchased along with smaller food items. A road-building crew had recently torn through her gate when they bulldozed the road, so it lay askew as I drove through. I knocked loudly. Naomi waved me inside. I introduced myself. She motioned me further inside, where she sank into a large cushioned chair and told me stories of her life as an educator for the community. She told me she was eighty-five and talked about her career as a teacher and how education was the most important thing a person could achieve. She talked about the importance of communication and the importance of teaching. My recorder was packed. The tape was silent. I asked if I could meet with her again and record what she knew of place names in and around Macy. She looked puzzled. Place names? She really didn't know any of those. It wasn't what she wanted to talk about. When I called her again on other occasions, she explained that there was someone else writing her life story. Life story? I had explained to her that I was after place names. I wondered at the direction this was heading. Why was I so insistent on a course of action that obviously was not taking place? The research about place names was going nowhere. What if I let things take their own path? What if I found women who wanted to talk about something else, something that pertained uniquely to them? Their life stories? I decided to let go and see what happened.

One of the first things that happened was an interview with Eleanor Baxter, now tribal vice-chair. In the elections that took place in November 2003, her office had changed. She was busier than ever but made time to see me. She told me about her grandmother, a medicine woman who wore the Mark of Honor, and said she would share pictures with me of her ancestors and family members.[6] We talked of other things pertaining to her life and her career in tribal politics. I asked if I could interview her for the project and she agreed. Over a period of several months, we met and talked. I recorded her stories along with those of Alice Saunsoci, the language teacher at the Nebraska Indian Community College. From there, I met Háwate, also named Wenona Caramony, through Vida Stabler, the language teacher at the Omaha Nation Public School. Vida had earlier given me Háwate's name and asked me to write her a letter, explaining that I was writing about women's life stories. I did so and waited to hear back. On a trip to Macy to meet with Eleanor, I was told that Háwate had been called away. I wanted to find out whether she got my letter or when she might be back. I looked for Alice at the NICC, but she was attending to the birth of her adopted daughter's child. Adrift, I went to the high school to try to catch Vida. She explained that Háwate had been out of town and was hard to reach. As we talked, Háwate suddenly walked in. Vida's eyes grew as wide as mine.

Folklorist and ethnithicist Dr. Barre Toelken told the story of his visit to a woman named Grandma Johnson in Navajo country, at a settlement called Westwater. He had been living and working with the Navajos and had left a month earlier, informing them that he would not return for some time. On a whim, he drove his parents from Salt Lake City to Blanding, a "tiny town in Utah's western edge" to introduce them to his Navajo family and friends. From there, they drove to Westwater and then to the hogan of Grandma Johnson. He said he could smell and see the juniper smoke from her fire. He went inside and found that there was "a large pot of coffee beside her, a stack of Navajo bread already made and a skillet with eight eggs sizzling on a raked-out bed of coals." He noted that Grandma Johnson spoke no English and had no electricity or phone and "no windows in her hogan through which she could have seen a car approaching in time to put eight eggs in the pan." He also said that no one else had arrived to tell her of the Toelken's pending arrival. Later that day, there was a sudden visit from a man known as Little Wagon, who had adopted Barre into his family. He had traveled from a place called Montezuma Creek, thirty miles south, and had left the previous day by burro—the same time Toelken and his parents left Salt Lake City. "I came over to meet your parents," he told him. "Such anecdotes," Toelken said, "abound in conversations and reminiscences of those who have spent considerable time in Indian country" (Walker 1995, 46–47).

I continued to have similar situations as Toelken. On another occasion, I could not find Alice and since she had no phone I did not know how to reach her. While contemplating a solution, she arrived and sat down as if she knew I had been looking for her. Another experience involved getting recommendations from Eleanor and Alice of other women elders who might be willing to visit with me. They both agreed that elder and Head Start leader Susan Fremont would be a possibility. I sent a letter to Susan introducing myself and letting her know that I hoped for an interview. Again, I sought Vida's help. When I walked into the language and culture center at the high school, she had been in conversation with a woman she introduced as Susan Fremont. Just as we were exchanging greetings, Háwate walked in, and Vida and I were able to set up a tentative appointment time for a recording session. It seemed as if everyone was there at the right moment.

Toelken spoke of this as a logic that is not linear in nature (Walker 1995, 48). Nebraska folklorist Roger Welsch was once invited to an Omaha Indian dance where he was to be head dancer. He was notified of the date but not the time or the place. He drove all over town, trying to find out where the dance was being held. He did find "one of the principal people" watching a baseball game. After the game, Welsch wanted to know where to go and what to do. The man responded, "Well, it looks like everyone came here. We might as well have the dance here" (49). Like Welsch, I felt we might as well "have the dance" in Vida's office.

Toelken referred to this phenomenon of apparent "supernatural communication" as "the moccasin telegraph" and told of a comment by Susie Yellowtail when he was invited to speak at Carroll College in Helena, Montana. He would be telling a coyote story "out of season," and the repercussions could be serious. Susie told him, "Yeah, go ahead. We need the rain anyway." Toelken wrote that this belief is widespread among Natives: stories are so powerful they can change the weather (53). As Thomas King wrote in *The Truth About Stories*, "Stories are wondrous things. And they are dangerous . . . you can't understand the world without telling a story" (8, 32).

After meeting Háwate, it seemed as though life stories would be the path my research would take. I think it had been the path all along.

Acknowledgments

This work owes much to the Omaha community in Macy as a whole, particularly the women who agreed to meet with me and let me hear their stories: Eleanor Baxter, Alice Saunsoci, and Háwate, Wenona Caramony. To these women I am grateful beyond words. *Wíbthaho^n*. They gave willingly of their time and assisted me in reviewing transcribed material. I additionally owe a debt of gratitude to the tribal council members and to Chairman Grant for meeting with me and helping me initially find ways to proceed with the project.

This work would not be complete without the skills and knowledge of those who helped me learn the Omaha language at the University of Nebraska–Lincoln: scholar and educator Dr. Mark Awakuni-Swetland; linguist Rory Larson; and Omaha speakers Emmaline Sanchez and Alberta Canby. I am especially indebted to these people, who spent many afternoons of hard work with us to review the language and to assist our class in whatever way they could. Their generosity and time are greatly appreciated. I would also like to recognize my fellow Omaha language classmates for their encouragement and for helping me to continue through four years of intensive language study: Kurt Kinbacher, Elaine Nelson, Carrie Wolfe, Mike Hammons, Megan Merrick, Jessica Waite, Andy Pedley, Sara Anderson, Loren Frerichs, and Matt Shumacher.

I am grateful to Vida Stabler, who teaches the Omaha language at the public school in Macy and runs the culture center there. She works with the elders in the community to record their stories and to digitize these stories for incorporation into the archives. Her assistance has been key in my research.

I would like to thank my husband, Reece Summers, for his company on many trips to Macy, for his patience in seeing me through this project, and for his many years of support in Arizona, Utah, and Nebraska to compete the PhD in English. I could not have done this without his emotional and financial support. Also, I would like to thank my children for their ongoing encouragement throughout: Stephanie, Shane, Josh, and Maya. I would also like to express my gratitude to my parents, Dr. Guy and Dorothy Matson, for their inspiration—that a mind at work, one that is always curious and looking for answers, is the greatest gift one could have.

To my friend and mentor, Dr. Fran Kaye, I express gratitude for her mentoring and intellectual skills that helped in the completion of this work. Thanks additionally to Dr. Tom Gannon and Dr. John Wunder for their time, review of material, and suggestions leading toward completion of this work.

Finally, this research would not have been possible without financial support from Grants-in-Aid for Graduate Students with the Center for Great Plains Studies, University of Nebraska–Lincoln, and a grant from the Charles Redd Center for Western Studies at Brigham Young University. I want to express my deepest thanks for their support. It is important to also mention the cooperation and approval of the Institutional Review Board at the University of Nebraska. During the research, reapplication to consider the change of topic was necessary. Throughout this process, the Board was extremely helpful.

Omaha Language Pronunciation Guide

Adapted and updated by Mark Awakuni-Swetland, with permission of the Umóⁿhoⁿ Language and Culture Center

Consonants
Consonants similar to English:

Writing symbol	Umó^{n}ho^n example	English example
b	búta (round)	boy
ch	chéshka (short)	church
d	dúba (four)	dog
g	gubéhi (hackberry tree)	girl
h	huhu (fish)	hi
m	mí (sun)	man
n	ní (water)	no
s	sábe (black)	sun
w	waskíthe (fruit)	wing
z	zí (yellow)	zoo
sh	shé (apple)	ship
zh	zhí^{n}ga (small)	beige
th	thawá (count)	that

Consonants somewhat like English:

In the Umó^{n}ho^n language, *p*, *t*, and *k* have two forms, where one is followed by a puff of air and the other is not. Those followed by a puff of air (you can feel it on your hand if you talk into your hand) sound like English *p*, *t*, and *k* at the beginning of words and are written with a superscript ^{h} after them. Those that are not followed by the puff of air (aspiration) sound almost like *b*, *d*, and *g* in English. They are similar to the *p*, *t*, and *k* in English when these sounds follow the sound s.

k	ké (turtle)	skip
k^h	k^{h}e ('the' inanimate horizontal)	kitten
p	péxe (gourd)	spot
p^h	p^{h}í (I went)	pot
t	té (buffalo)	stop
t^h	t^{h}e ('the' inanimate vertical or set)	top
ch^h	mo^{n}ch^{h}ú (grizzly bear)	chop

Consonants different from English:

| x | xúde (gray) | Ba**ch** said forcefully |
| x | xagé (to cry) | Ba**ch** said softly |

'x' is not an English sound, but it is not difficult to make. You can feel the vibration at the back of your tongue behind the part you use to make a 'k' sound.

| ' | wa'ú (woman) | uh-oh |

' creates a break between two sounds. It is called a glottal stop because it stops the sounds in your throat. It is the sound that is made between 'uh' and 'oh' in 'uh-oh' in English.

p'	p'útho^n	steam
t'	hó^{n}t'ega	house fly
s'	s'áthe	sour
sh'	i^{n}sh'áge	elder male

' can also follow consonants such as *p*, *t*, *s*, and *sh*. Here, it creates a stop after that consonant and then the air is released before the vowel. These are called ejectives because the air ejects out of the mouth when it is released after stopping.

Vowels

Umón̄hon̄ has its own set of vowel sounds. *Vowels* are sounds that are pronounced with the mouth relatively open. With consonants, the tongue or mouth either stops the air (for example t or m) or makes the air rough (s, sh). With vowels, the air escapes easily.

Oral vowel sounds similar to those in English:

a	ská (white)	f**a**ther
e	shé (apple)	w**ei**ght, Las V**e**gas
i	niní (tobacco)	rad**i**o
o	ahó (hello, Male speaker only)	**o**kay, b**o**at
u	tú (blue)	bl**ue**

Nasal vowel sounds:

on̄   ón̄hon̄ (yes)   **lawn**

You can practice making this sound by starting to say 'on' and drawing out the vowel for a long time. It is this sound of the vowel (before you say the consonant –n that is made by on̄.

in̄   wín̄ (one)   **mean**

This sound can be practice by saying 'mean' and similarly drawing out the vowel as you did for 'on̄.'

Vowel lengthening:

Umóⁿhoⁿ has several words with a longer-sounding vowel just like the English word 'Wow!' when the vowel is drawn out in an exclamation of surprise.

Vowel length can change the meaning of a word. We mark the longer vowels, both oral and nasal, by doubling the vowel. Be careful not to pronounce the second vowel as a separate syllable. Instead, just pronounce both as a single, long length sound.

níde	buttocks
níide	cooked, well done
nóⁿde	wall
nóⁿoⁿde	heart

Women Elders' Life Stories of the Omaha Tribe

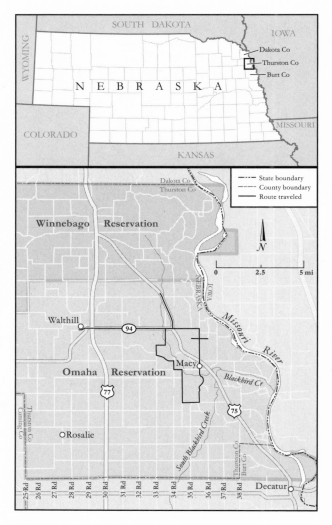

The Omaha Indian Reservation is located in southeast Thurston County, Nebraska. The dark section highlighted on the map is the route Eleanor Baxter and the author took while driving around Macy. Walthill is north and west of Macy on Highway 94.

1. Finding the Sacred

In the spring of 2005, Omaha tribal member Eleanor Baxter and I got into her car and headed north from the tribal council building in Macy, Nebraska. The day was warm. Spring grasses grew along the banks and high hills surrounding the reservation. Earlier, Eleanor had talked about taking me on a tour of the Macy Reservation. That morning seemed like the right time. "I'm going to take you to our cemetery," she said. I had passed this cemetery many times heading toward the town of Macy from the north. It was on my left as I headed downhill to the main area of the reservation. But this was only a part of the reservation, which was surrounded by rolling hills and verdant with new crop growth, raspberry bushes, and giant cottonwoods hugging the Missouri River. Not far from Macy was Big Elk Park, marked by lush wooded hills and a rich canopy of trees. Houses dotted the landscape in all directions, set on the land in circular patterns that led back to the town. The cemetery always caught my eye. It was placed on a hilltop overlooking the council building, the C-Store, the rows of houses, and the senior center. It was a marker against time. Eleanor had spent her early childhood in Macy before moving to Lincoln as a young girl, and as she talked I heard in her voice the tug of emotion and connection to land and place that now informed her life.

That morning, before we left the council building for the "tour," Eleanor told me the story of a young woman whose car had careened off the highway heading east from Walthill earlier in the week, killing her. The woman left a grandmother, a husband, and small children. There was to be a funeral later that morning. "I've got time to show you around before everything starts," she said. She took me over to the community center where the funeral was to be held. I met the grandmother, stoic in her grief. She had lost a son earlier that year. The deaths seemed too many to endure. So it seemed ironic to begin at the cemetery where there was so much sorrow. Yet starting where ancestors and family were buried seemed appropriate when it came to returning to one's roots and the place of one's birth, paying homage to those who went before. It was sacred landscape.

Eleanor pointed to a fresh mound outside the car window. "That's where the girl will be buried and that's where Timothy Saunsoci is buried. He was a young man of twenty-three—came home from Lincoln at seventeen, and then my parents raised him. He had three kids and was killed. There's not a day that goes by that I don't think of him because he was . . . he hurt us all so badly because of the love we had for him." The word "home" resonated. Lincoln was not home, even though he had lived there. Macy was.

Caretakers could no longer take care of the graves because of money shortages. Eleanor said they did have people who cared for them, however. "Years ago they had old timers.

When there was a death, there was a group of men that used to just automatically go. Everything was done. They just went and did it out of the goodness of their heart. These are all my family here—my mother, Mae Blackbird Saunsoci." She asked me to look carefully at the gravestones. They had tipis on them. She pointed to where her father, Oliver, was buried. "He was what they call a road man—a minister in the Native American Church. He officiated at all the birthdays and dinners and burials."

The car wove along the roads that marked the circles of mounds. Eleanor said that mounds were a part of their culture, that it seemed strange to have everything flat. She took me to an old part of the cemetery where her grandparents were buried. I took pictures of some of the old stones, which dated back to the early 1800s. Uphill from these old markers was Military Circle, profuse with graves. Eleanor told me about the time she was a speaker on a panel and was asked by a "young lady" what her people had contributed to the United States. "I could've went off on a tangent because . . . I just told them in a way that we contributed to the government, gave them our land. We didn't give them our land. It was taken from us. We served in all the wars. All the wars! And this Military Circle is where our veterans are." There were fresh mounds among the old. "See all the mounds? Those are the ones that died."

> *This is sacred land, she said.*
> *She was a wise woman*
> *Who was very old.*
> *Maybe Grandmother Spider.*
> *I saw her in my dreams, when she came to me*
> *   with eyes round and hard*

Cold and dark.
The voices of the land were everywhere,
In trees, in grass blades, in houses.
They were everywhere, these voices.
Hushed into sacred places, in roots of trees,
    in soil and wind.
Water.
When the government took the land
They took the blood and bones of ancestors
    lying deep in the earth.
Took them without thinking of the consequences.
She stopped to look at me with eyes gone black
Raven eyes,
Turned inward
Into the blue-tipped wings,
Seeing into orbs of silence
Where blood runs in rivers
And cries are still heard echoing in canyons,
Secret places.
Ancient sorrows run deep.
I heard the blackbirds rise from the branches,
circle the land.
Once the sacredness is stolen, she said
It is over.

Eleanor and I left the cemetery and drove downhill toward what she called HUD housing, an urban development federal program. "Here is Tower Hill. This is where we begin to get street names. We're doing that because we have to have physical addresses now instead of using post office boxes. It used to be called ADC, Aid to Dependent Children Hill. That's just how Indian humor is," she said. "They can pick on each other the worst. And these are some of the housing circles. Some of the housing units here were just remodeled so they look pretty good."

One housing circle was called Thunder Circle. I asked who picked the names. She told me her daughter, Shannon, had been one of those who helped pick names and that two or three people get to decide. "These are all the Fanny Mae and HUD housing units. Eighteen more units are going to be built." We left the housing area and headed into the rural countryside. "There's people buried all over the reservation," Eleanor said. "That's the way it was done back in the days of the prairie." The land stretched to the horizon, open and undulating. The bones of the people that lay on this land anchored it as a kind of talisman against land losses and future depredations—well known to the Omaha. "This is our land here," Eleanor said as we drove. "I can truly say that this is our reservation because we weren't removed. This is our land here. When I came back, I had to know. I knew I was Indian and I knew where I came from, but to go back to history I had to relearn again and know dates and time."

We circled around from a more rural area to the southeast, past more houses to what was termed the "horse project." Eleanor said it was for the kids, to help them with emotional problems. She explained that the kids take care of the horses and learn to ride them. We turned and drove north, uphill to a brick building. "This is our local college, NICC," she said. "Nebraska Indian Community College. It's accredited now. Alice [Saunsoci] teaches language there." Downhill from NICC were more houses, what Eleanor called the West Projects. I asked her if she felt reconnected with Omaha tradition and culture since she had moved back from Lincoln much later in her life. "I was always in it anyway. It was one thing I never lost was the customs, the traditions, the way we live. I never lost that thought." We turned west and headed out from Yellow Smoke Road to the Bureau roads.

The car tires stirred up dust, which lingered on the edges of the glass and in the cracks of the doors. I wished for rain. But now, the hills were beginning to show green and the ditches were full of raspberry bushes. We were north of Yellow Smoke Road. "There's all kinds of shortcuts to get to Highway 77," she said. "Any road you take west is going to lead you. When we were kids, this whole creek here, Blackbird Creek, it widens. And this is where I grew up, around this area before we moved to Lincoln. Back then, we didn't have bicycles—anything. Everything we did was walk. Walk, walk, walk. And our food was squirrels, rabbits, and even raccoons." She said her brothers were the hunters. The trees, which they cut for their wood stoves, kept them warm in the winter. "Everybody had a wood stove. We didn't have gas—electricity. We had lamps. These creeks here, we used to pick gooseberries. Raspberries. And look for morel mushrooms—and you can dry those. They're found all over. All over. Sometimes I can remember there were so many mushrooms. I can remember filling baths and tubs and everything up with mushrooms. Then we'd dry them. They'd shrivel up to marble size. This was our play area when were small."

Raspberry and gooseberry bushes grew thick along Blackbird Creek. Eleanor cautioned me about poison ivy. Houses were scattered at different points on the hillsides. She pointed out where some once stood that were now gone and others that remained solidly on the land. "This was my stomping grounds," she reminisced. I heard the longing in her voice.

We stopped at the place where she was born, a two-story wood frame house on the corner of the Bureau roads. Some of her family relations came out to see who had pulled in the driveway. We visited briefly while two dogs, eager for attention, circled around me. Conversation died away. Eleanor got back in the car and I jumped in beside her. This time we headed west, toward Black Elk Park, toward the old Mission School. "I would take you up there but it looks pretty rough. If you go right over the trees there, there are some old gravestones and there's a foundation where the school was and the first time I . . ." Her voice trailed off. "When I moved back, I told my husband, 'Take me up there.' When I got up there I felt the most peaceful feeling of serenity. And I'd read Francis La Flesche's book *The Middle Five* [about boarding schools to "civilize" Indians] and I wanted to go up there. I envisioned all the little kids just running around up there and I thought, boy, you could get lost in a time capsule up here. I felt peaceful. Other people have told me they felt real uncomfortable and had to get out of there."

> *The Old Mission School has long since disappeared,*
> *The woman told me,*
> *The one with the hard black eyes*
>   *that had seen every-thing.*
> *She showed me around in my dreams.*
> *There is only this old stone foundation,*
>   *this line of stones.*
> *She pointed. But there is where the fireplace stood.*
> *Maybe that's where it was.*
> *I don't remember. I was only a girl then.*
> *They cut your hair at boarding schools and*
>   *put you in strange clothes*

*And said you could never speak your
    native language again.
They stole that from us—the language
    along with the land.
They beat it out of us.
They watched as our skin lay in shreds on the ground,
And then they kicked it into dust.
Then when it was all said and done,
We went home to the reservation and didn't know
    what it was like to be Indian.
Now we are trying to catch up, trying to
    resurrect those things
That were so important to us.
You know,
When they take your soul, what's left?*

Eleanor showed me where an old house used to be, down-hill and to the west of the mission site, in a grove of trees and bushes. She pointed ahead to a winding dirt road, deeply rutted. "This led up to the Holy Fire Place. The Holy Fire Place is where our people used to go and fast. And we were told not to go up there because it was sacred ground. It's all fenced off." She said that people still go there to look off the bluff that looks down into the Hole in the Rock.

The Holy Fire Place is located along the Missouri Bluffs not far from Council Point and is considered a sacred spot where the forefathers handed down Omaha ceremonies. Stabler discussed Omaha legend connected to this spot. The people were old and poor and wished to gain strength through prayers to Wakónda. They took their young boys (about twelve or thirteen years old) to a hill to pray for four days without eating or drinking. On the fourth day, at the height of weakness, a vision or dream was given to those who had endured the ritual of fasting and praying. A song was associated with this vision. The song "became a medium of communication between the visionary and the object of his dream. Throughout his life, this dream or vision and the song became his help and strength in the hour of need" (Stabler 1943, 38–41). After the vision, which is referred to as No^{n}zhi^n zho^n ("to stand sleeping"), the youth returned to his family but remained solitary, eating and resting. After the fourth day, the vision was shared with an old man who had experienced a similar vision. If the youth spoke of the vision before the four days, it would be lost to him (41–42). Stabler reinforced how this ritual brought communion with Wakó^{n}da, the Great Spirit.

Eleanor drove into the parking lot of the tribal council building. She parked the car and said she had to prepare for the funeral of the girl who had recently died. I thanked her for the time we spent together that morning and watched her walk away from me. From inside the community center came the sound of the drums and voices rising and falling like soft ripples on Blackbird Creek as it wound through the hills.

On May 16, 2005, I returned to Macy to visit with Omaha language teacher Alice Saunsoci. We met at the Omaha tribal council building. She wanted to drive out into the countryside to show me her old childhood school—McCauley. By now, the land around Macy was alive with color. The prairie grasses, deep green and purple, blew in the spring winds. I could feel their energy as a palpable presence.

As we headed west, the land stretched behind us. Raspberry and gooseberry bushes were coming to life in the ditches and along the edges of the road. Alice commented that no one ate them anymore because of all the herbicides and chemicals

farmers used on their fields. I remembered Eleanor's childhood stories of gathering berries and eating them and felt
saddened by the loss of such food. We drove south and then
east, past the old school. I took a picture. The school bell,
once anchored in the ruins, was missing, the windows gaping
and empty like hollow eye sockets. But the charm remained.
It was near a creek where Alice said she and her friends used
to play. She talked about the neighbors she remembered, the
German family across from her grandfather's place who were
long gone. She explained how she didn't live with her father
and stepmother. But they were close by, so she did go there
to help with chores or to visit.

I am reminded of the first time I met Alice and she talked
about her return to the land, to the home place of Macy from
Lincoln where she had lived since 1965. Her husband, Frank,
was ill and told the family he wanted to go home. He said,
"We're going to go back to Macy—to survive." After the
move, she attended the Nebraska Indian Community College in Macy and graduated in 1991. Her speech instructor
asked her what she wanted to do in ten years. "I said that ten
years from now, I want to come back as a speaker, keynote
speaker, and I also want to serve on the board of directors,
board of trustees at the college. Thirteen years later, I'm on
the board and I was a keynote speaker."

I got out of the car and took a picture of McCauley. Alice
stood next to me. Alice said she has good memories of her
rural childhood in Macy and that she will always treasure
memories of her grandparents. But the area has changed sig-
nificantly. The children she went to school with are now "scattered about." Many of the farmers in that area lost their land
and moved to the city of Omaha to survive. One of these

families used to live across from her. Her memories are framed by those no longer there—those who moved on and have left behind shadows of their childhood experiences.

We stood for a few more minutes, feeling the wind on our faces. It's harsher now, pressing the grasses flat and rattling the dry cornstalks from last year's planting. "One of these days—she might be alive or maybe she isn't," Alice said. "Maybe I walk past her and don't know it. But she was my teacher and all of us that were there, we never called her Miss Ferguson, we called her Punkie because that was her name. So one of these days, maybe I'll run into Punkie."

The drive ended at Alice's house east of Macy. It was a rectangular brick home with the poles of a sweat lodge in the yard. She showed me where she wanted a garden but commented that it was too overgrown with weeds. The farmer, she explained, who could plow it for her and turn the soil had not shown up to help. I asked if I could take her picture. She walked over and stood under a tree next to her house. Her lips moved silently as the camera button clicked.

> *Alice stands under that tree in the late spring*
> *The one with leaves just coming out, catching the wind*
> *She's in Levis and has a wool coat on with colored*
>   *geometric designs.*
> *Her gray-black hair is sleek, shiny, pulled back into*
>   *a long braid.*
> *She is regal.*
> *The breeze catches the edge of her coat,*
>   *makes creases in her jeans.*
> *Her dark eyes look back at me as I catch*
>   *her image in the viewfinder.*

The square shape of the camera window
    brings her into focus.
With a click she is imprinted forever.
But I see her spirit there, flying over the trees
Laughing
She is the sky.

Later, I would come to know another elder—Háwate, also named Wenona Caramony. She also had returned to Macy as an older woman and assisted the Omaha community as an educator and language teacher. But when I held Alice's image in the frame of the camera, I thought of only one thing: in return there is rebirth. Sacred landscape—land imbued with spiritual presence through these women's stories, beyond physicality into sacrality. Landscape is the thread that combines the elements of storytelling and is a way of preserving cultural and spiritual life and survival.

I take a shortcut to Highway 77 along Yellow Smoke Road. The dust grinds beneath the tires and spins underneath, leaving small brown whirlpools.

Earth
Being
I search for you
In the stories of women everywhere.
In the cloth of women's lives—shared and
    unabated callings that speak of
Crossings
Comings and goings
Homeland.
Úzhetha

In Omaha language
Means weary.
I am weary
Of the crossings
But in return there is hope.

2. Language as Landscape

Ethnic identity is twin skin to linguistic identity—I am my language. Until I can take pride in my language, I cannot take pride in myself. | GLORIA ANZALDUA

Alice Saunsoci talked about her indigenous roots with pride. Her grandparents in Macy had a large garden where they raised much of their food. They had horses, chickens, and hogs. The grandmother spoke only Omaha. Her grandfather, John, went to Carlisle Indian School, so he knew English. He translated for the grandmother. But the grandmother was suspicious of white people and insisted that only the Omaha language be spoken in the household. Alice told me her people were experiencing a breakdown. She talked about the severity of oppression by the United States government. She referred to this as "victimization." Boarding schools to assimilate and acculturate Indian children became rampant government policy (in 1879), and diseases that they weren't immune to created horrific suffering and population losses. Among these diseases were smallpox, measles, and tuberculosis. Alice's mother died of tuberculosis when she was twenty-six. "I didn't know her," she said. Yet she explained that today she has more understanding of what took place and has no hate. Survival is paramount. She talked about the "coming days of our ancestors"—what is known to her as the significant roles her grandmother and mother played to survive. They had large gardens, made food, and raised children—no different from what she is doing today.

Alice said their language was going to survive. The Omaha language is thriving and growing—thanks to language teachers like Alice, Háwate, and teacher Vida Stabler at the Umón-hon Nation Public School. "We have people in our community right now who are interested in our language. They want to learn. And it's easier for us, for me, because we teach the Omaha language scientifically. We have our lesson plans at NICC and that's how we do it."

Vida Stabler has developed an archival language base at the school and established a culture center there where the Omaha language is spoken and learned by the youth. The elders are active in helping the young people learn the language. Vida records the language as spoken by the elders on CDs for future generations to draw on. She said, "Some of our young people go off and go to school, then make their way back. Some try to go to college. They go through culture shock and come back within a half-year or so. Then some probably manage both lives." Language is paramount in maintaining and preserving Omaha culture and traditions. Háwate said the younger generations are aware of the importance of education. She emphasized the importance of language preservation. She said there is a large gap between what she termed "speakers, nonspeakers, and active listeners"—those who understand the language but don't speak it. Her goal as a language advocate is to "bring them to speech" and give them opportunities to learn the language in all of its various forms. Her primary goal is to work with the children—to instill in them the vitality and importance of learning their native language.

Sacred Landscape

Beginnings are told through language. The land is made sacred through stories that speak of the Omaha Sacred Legend, which tells that people once lived in water (see Fletcher and La Flesche 1911, 70–71). When they opened their eyes, they could see nothing—hence the name Niádi i^{n}shtágabtha, or "eyes open in the water." As the people emerged from the water and beheld day, the child name Kétha gaxe was given—"to make or behold the clear sky." They were naked but not ashamed. As time passed, oral legend says they desired "coverings" that they made from weed and grass fiber. The people lived near a large body of water in a "wooded country" where they hunted deer with clubs. As they wandered around the shores of this great body of water, they grew cold and were poor. They found a bluish stone and began chipping it to make knives and arrowheads. But the cold continued to plague them. Then a man found a dry elm stick, placed it in a hole in the ground, and rubbed it with another stick. Smoke emanated from the sticks. The people smelled the smoke and came to watch and help rub the sticks together. The fire erupted and they now were warm and could cook their food. They built grass shelters with the shoulder blade of a deer.

After a time, the legend said, the people grew tired of only roasting their meat and desired another way to cook it. A man found some clay that mixed well with sand and molded it into a vessel. He added grass, set the vessel on it, and lit a fire until the clay grew hard. He then added water inside the vessel, which held. Meat was added to the water. This way, the people could also eat boiled meat. The grass clothing they wore would fuzz and drop off. They wanted something different so they used their stone knives to scrape the hides they previously had thrown away. The people made the hides soft and pliable with their hands and then made the hides into clothing. Oral legend says that stone axes were made to help the women break dry wood for the fires. These axes had a groove for the handle and were fastened together with rawhide. To further help in cutting wood, they made wedges of stone or iron to split logs. Bark shelters were substituted for grass. The people then put deer and elk skins on the poles, but the deer skins were too small and the elk skins grew hard and unmanageable so they returned to bark coverings. Later, buffalo hides were used to make "good tents." Leg bones of deer were used to make awls, sew sinew, and make these coverings for their homes (Fletcher and La Flesche 1911, 71).

> *There is another story told by the elders and others.*
> *This is how it goes.*
> *In the creation story of the Omaha people's*
>   *Pebble Society*
> *Land was the bringer and giver of life.*
> *Spirits descended from the air and became*
>   *flesh and blood.*

They fed on grass seeds and fruit from trees.
It was said that the land, the sacred land,
    vibrated with expressions of joy
To the creator, the maker of all things— Wakŏⁿda.
This story—it tells about how the people
    were full of sorrow.
The First Spirit spoke to them and said that
    toward the coming of the sun
Where all creatures were gathered,
People, animals, insects—all things,
There was a creature that was the greatest of all—the
    Great White Rock.
It was as high as the heavens.
An Omaha Creation hymn expresses the sacredness
    of land and place.
This hymn rises to the high powers: the sun, moon,
    sky, earth, the winds
Of the four corners.
The rock on which creation was centered.
(Olson 1979, 1–2, 60; poetic interpretation by the author)

According to Omaha tribal tradition, the original homeland of the Omaha was in the Ohio River Valley. They are
part of the Siouan language group—the Dhégiha—which in-
cluded the Ponca, Quapaw, Kansa, and Osage. These tribes
were located in the Middle Mississippian culture flourishing in the vicinity of St. Louis from approximately 800 to
1400 AD (Omaha Tribe of Nebraska 2000, 4). This heartland
area was comprised of what is now called Indiana and Kentucky "at the mouth of the Wabash." Sometime around 1400
to 1700, tribes known as the Five Cognate Tribes (Omaha,
Ponca, Quapaw, Kansa, and Otoe) moved westward toward

the Mississippi River. The Quapaw moved south to the Arkansas River, arriving between 1541 and 1643. The others moved northward, the Omahas "going against the current." The Osage and Kansa traveled up the Missouri River, where they settled in their present homeland around 1700. The Omahas and Poncas traveled farther north, up the Des Moines River, where they associated with the Ioway tribe of that region (Myers 1992, 4).

As the Omaha migrated from their ancestral homelands, they needed something to anchor them and hold them together, something to establish tribal unity. They wanted a symbol that would bind and unite them collectively. "Umóⁿhoⁿxti" did this. Considered a living entity, Umóⁿhoⁿxti, otherwise known as the Sacred Pole or Venerable Man, became a center around which Omaha life was focused.

> *An Edenic symbol exists*
> *Of their journey. It is called*
> *The Sacred Pole.*
> *The way the story goes is that there was this young man.*
> *He got lost in the forest while tribal elders were*
> *   at a meeting.*
> *This meeting, á-biama, they say, was to resolve how*
> *   to face new challenges,*
> *Ensure tribal unity while migrating into these places*
> *Now known as northern Iowa and*
> *Southern Minnesota.*
> *All this took place from the Ohio Valley region.*
> *So this young man, he was walking along and he saw*
> *   a brilliant light*
> *Coming from a tree.*

This was a cottonwood.

And he watched it for two nights. Then he went back
and told the elders,

Those at the tribal meeting. Hey, he says, I saw this tree.
It was all lit up.

I couldn't look at it, it was so lit up. The elders said,
á-biama,

"How could this be?"

They didn't really believe him. So they decided to go
look at it.

Sure enough, they saw it too. There were also tracks
of animals

All sorts of animals making paths leading to this tree.

The creatures had rubbed against the bark and
polished it.

The elders said to themselves, "This is a gift from
Wakóⁿda, the creator.

This is the symbol that we will take with us on our
journey."

They brought the tree back to the tribe dressed like
a man.

The way the story goes is that the tree from then on
belonged to the people,

All the people, as a whole—not to a particular
individual.

It was symbolic of the importance and vitality of the
Omaha communal life.

The elders and all the people,

They agreed that everyone should bring their problems
to the pole

And in accordance with tribal custom present gifts to it.

The Omaha said it was a sentient being, given to them
*   when they needed*
Something to unite them.
It was given supernatural sanction,
It belonged to them as a sacred symbol, a living entity
From which they could gather strength.
It was honored in the Moon When the Buffalo Bellow
*   and it was central*
In uniting the Omaha as they headed toward the
*   plains,*
And later
Up the Missouri River.
That's the way the story goes
And is told today.
(Myers 1992, 7; poetic interpretation by the author)

Missionary-ethnologist James Owen Dorsey, in the latter part of the nineteenth century, noted in *Omaha Sociology* that the Sacred Pole was originally longer that it is in its present state. "The lower part having worn out, a piece of ash-wood about 18 inches long has been fastened to the cottonwood with a soft piece of cord made of a buffalo hide. The ash-wood forms the bottom of the pole and is the part stuck in the ground at certain times. The cottonwood is about 8 feet long" (234).

The physical presence of Umó^{n}ho^{n}ti changed in the nineteenth century as Indians were systematically placed on reservations. Dispossession of sacred objects from traditional keepers to museums became commonplace. This was evident when the Sacred Pole was removed from its keeper, Yellow Smoke. The name, according to Dorsey, referred originally to the Sacred

Pole. "The proper name, 'Yellow Smoke,' 'Smoked Yellow,' or Cude-nazi [sic], also refers to the pole which has become 'yellow from smoke'" (Dorsey, *Omaha Sociology*, quoted in Ridington and Hastings 1997, 234). Yellow Smoke was also the name of the last keeper of the Sacred Pole, Shúdenazi, or Robert Morris, a member of the Hó^{n}ga clan. "Shúdenazi" refers to a title rather than name: "It refers to the keeper as being smoked with age like the pole himself" (xix).

The possession and subsequent transfer of the Sacred Pole to the Peabody Museum in Boston in 1888 was rife with controversy. At the time, a white woman, Alice Fletcher, and Omaha tribal member Francis La Flesche were working collectively as ethnographers, obtaining stories, songs, traditions, customs, and other ethnographic data regarding the tribe's history and ceremonies. Their work was published in 1911 in two volumes entitled *The Omaha Tribe*. During the later part of the nineteenth century, when Fletcher and La Flesche were collaborating on *The Omaha Tribe*, complete assimilation of Indians into the dominant Euroamerican culture was mandated, and the means to carry this out resulted in placing Indian children in boarding schools where they could be Christianized and "made white." La Flesche himself attended the Mission School on the Omaha reservation when he was a boy. These boyhood experiences were later recounted in his book *The Middle Five*. Reformers at this time were represented as "benevolent" and as having the best interest of the Indians at heart. In reality, "the reformers had no qualms about using coercion to impose their notion of progress on aboriginal people" (Ridington and Hastings 1997, 12).

Alice Fletcher later became involved in the allotment program for Indians in which land was held in severalty or individual ownership. The harsh and tragic reality of allotment meant that Native lands passed rapidly into the hands of non-Native settlers, and land losses were rampant. Omahas today consider Fletcher's involvement in allotments to be "instruments of oppression and loss" (Ridington and Hastings 1997, 10). Part of these losses entailed the transfer of sacred objects to museums, including the Sacred Pole. Ridington stated in *Blessing for a Long Time* that "Omahas remember the 1880s as a time when the Tent of War, the Sacred Pole, the White Buffalo Hide, and other religious objects and their ceremonies were stolen from them. They are correct in identifying Fletcher and La Flesche as being responsible for these objects leaving tribal control. A key to their work was the transformation of sacred objects into ethnological specimens" (10). Ridington also noted that both Fletcher and La Flesche were "products of their time, each one coming to the ethnographic work they undertook together by the energy of opposite and sometimes fiercely competing cultural forces" (17).

Despite their joint work to record and preserve Omaha history and ceremonies, what remained was the manner the Sacred Pole was removed from Yellow Smoke's possession and placed in the Peabody Museum. "Omahas today are certain," Ridington wrote, "that Fletcher and La Flesche stole the Sacred Pole, or at least obtained it through coercion" (19). Doran Morris, Yellow Smoke's great-great-grandson, told Ridington that a part of their tribal history includes the belief that La Flesche took the pole when only the keeper's wife was at home. Fletcher wrote to the director of the Peabody Museum that La Flesche had "secured" the Sacred Pole and that it was a "great prize. It cost forty-five dollars and it is cheap" (quoted in Ridington and Hastings 89).

Ultimately, Ridington concluded that La Flesche did the right thing, "although perhaps in the wrong way for the wrong reasons. I would like to think, too, that the Pole himself saw fit to choose Francis as a respectful substitute for his traditional keeper in a time of crisis, as he seems to have chosen Doran Morris and [tribal historian] Dennis Hastings in our own time" (88). What needs to be considered overall is the era in which Fletcher and La Flesche were seeking transfer of sacred objects. At this particular juncture in history, it was believed by some Omaha progressives that the only way to preserve these objects was to transfer them into what they considered the safekeeping of museums. When allotment was rapidly taking place in the 1880s, land losses for the Omaha were staggering; an additional consequence was the possible disappearance of sacred objects.

Omaha Clans

"The Omaha now have seven clans," Eleanor said when I talked with her at the tribal council building. "My mother was from the Mo^{n}thí^{n}kagaxe clan. She was from the Earth People. My grandmother was Hó^{n}ga. My great-great-grandfather, his name was Yellow Smoke. When I found that out I was quite amazed because my mother never talked about that. There was a picture of him, and I have a picture of my grandfather. Yellow Smoke had four children—Cora, my grandmother Maggie, Carrie, and then they had a son named Tom. We used to call him Grandpa Tom because he was the son of Yellow Smoke."

Inside the council building seven brightly colored poles are arranged in a circle with the clan names and symbols marked on each pole. It was with reverence and respect that

I studied these whenever I was in the building to talk with Eleanor or Alice. (I met Háwate at the high school culture center.) In Dorsey's study of the Omaha, *Omaha Sociology*, he noted the placement of the clans within the hunting circle, the Húthuga. "In this circle, the gentes took their regular places pitching their tents, one after another, within the area necessary for each gens. This circle was not made by measurement, nor did anyone give direction where each tent should be placed; that was left to the women . . . the crier used to tell the people to what place they were to go, and when they reached it, the women began to pitch the tents" (219). When the Omaha went on the buffalo hunt for the last time in 1871–72, Dorsey recorded an account of the numbers of tents from Wahó^{n}thi^{n}ge, the chief of the Tesinde gens, to be 133 tents in the "Hangacenu" portion of the hunting circle and 147 tents in the "Inctasande" portion of the circle (219–20).

The hunting circle, known as Húthuga, or the Omaha Tribal Form, was a reflection of spiritual cosmology and beliefs. The Omaha, as well as the Ponca and Osage, regarded life as a union between sky and earth forces. This union, the combining of the opposite or "cosmic powers," established laws to be obeyed, "a course he [an Omaha man] must follow if he would secure the continuation of his own life and the perpetuation of his tribe—a law which made exogamy a practical expression of this belief" (Fletcher and La Flesche 1911, 140). Tribes of the Dhégiha linguistic stock (Ponca, Osage, Quapaw, and Omaha) held these beliefs in common. The hunting circle symbolically reflected this belief system of the two separate but connected cosmic forces. The ideas symbolized by the Sky People were called the I^{n}shtásu^{n}da; the other half was named the Ho^{n}gashenu and was known as the Earth

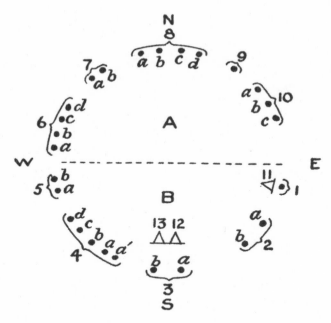

Omaha Hu'thuga, ceremonial encampment circle during the annual buffalo hunt.

People. "Here again," wrote Fletcher and La Flesche, "we find the tribal order standing for the union of sky and earth, the masculine and feminine forces from whose union all living things arise" (141). The southern half of the circle, the Earth People, had charge of the physical welfare of the tribe. The northern half of the circle, the Sky People, were in charge of rites connected to creation, the stars, and manifestations of the cosmic forces of life (195). There were five gens in each half, ten gens altogether. When Dr. Robin Ridington spoke to the Omaha during their 1988 powwow in the "sacred circle of oak trees," he addressed and acknowledged the two cosmologies reflected in the tribal circle. "Ahó! I^{n}shtásu^{n}da, Hó^{n}gashenu, tí agthó^n kahó^n," he began: "Hello I^{n}shtásu^{n}da, Sky People,

Hó^{n}gashenu, Earth People. I greet you as both sides of a single house joined here together as one people, one tribe in the sacred arena, just as they did long ago, in the Húthuga—the camp circle" (Ridington and Hastings 36).

Within this circle, clan responsibilities governed the "fundamental realities" of the Omaha people—tribal responsibilities and marriage relationships. The axis of the Omaha tribal circle is east-west, following the path of the sun and divided into northern and southern divisions. The northern division is comprised of Mo^{n}thí^{n}kagaxe, Tesí^{n}de, Tapá, I^{n}gthézhide, and I^{n}shtásu^{n}da. The southern division contains Kó^{n}ze, Thátada, Ho^{n}ga, I^{n}k^{h}ésabe, and Wézhi^{n}shte. Both divisions represent male–female principles and the balance of the universe (Myers 1992, 5–6).

In childhood, we are told that our language is wrong. Repeated attacks on our native tongue diminish our sense of self. The attacks continue throughout lives. | GLORIA ANZALDUA

Stories frame continued existence. Language, oral and written, testifies to the sacredness that is both land and self. The three women I spoke with about their lives all agreed that survivance is about language, about a return home to one's place of birth. Land is essence—both supra-real and real. It is surreal in the poetic form of storytelling where self is anchored to earth, to soil, to sacredness based on presence in the land. Land is the breath of life. Without it, spiritual energy is lost. Land is spun into chaos when greed for space means acquiring more and more land, regardless of consequences to all the energies of being—animate and inanimate.

Language survival is key in Alice Saunsoci's life; it connects two worlds where English is spoken but also Omaha.

On one occasion, we stood near the Missouri River at Black Elk Park while she talked about the time she brought her language students from the Nebraska Indian Community College to the park to hunt for mushrooms and talk in the Omaha language about their experience. Both aspects of learning the language were connected—food from the earth and its expression in language. The Missouri River moved along the bank, the water gray-green. The giant cottonwoods stood like river sentinels—guides to river travel. There was a sense of timelessness, of space.

> Integration Is about Stories
> *This is what Eleanor, Alice, and Háwate taught me.*
> *They taught me about the land and their*
> *place in this land.*
> *This is where creation begins and ends.*
> *It is a place of challenges, of dark and light*
> *stripped of color.*
> *It is a place of reality and dreams.*
> *Death—skeletal and deep*
> *And life that continues.*
> *Washkóⁿ*
> *Be strong, they told me.*
> *In their story is hope.*
> *Spaces in between words,*
> *Stories that defy difference.*
> *But anchor one into being.*

Alice Saunsoci in the backyard of her home in Macy.

Háwate after the interview at the Umóⁿhoⁿ Nation Public School. She is pictured here in the culture center wrapped in the blanket her mother made.

A signpost on a road near Macy seen while driving with Tribal Chairperson Eleanor Baxter.

One of the roads around Macy.

Macy countryside.

An old gravestone marker in the Macy cemetery.

Old gravestone markers, Macy cemetery.

The Missouri River near Macy.

Big Elk Park, Macy.

Big Elk Park, Macy.

The countryside near Macy seen while driving with Eleanor Baxter and
Alice Saunsoci.

Umóⁿhoⁿ Nation Public School, where Háwate was interviewed. The culture center, a circular room, is to the far left.

McCauley School, south of Macy, where Alice Saunsoci went to school as a young girl.

Eleanor Baxter's home and playground as a child in Macy. To the left
(not in the picture) is the creek where she played.

The west side of Eleanor Baxter's home, Macy.

UNL Omaha language class. Left to right: Loren Frerichs, Mike Hammons, Andy Pedley, Elaine Nelson, Matt Schumacher, Jessica Waite, Carrie Wolfe, Anna Ramsey, Megan Merrick, Kurt Kinbacher, and Omaha elder and speaker, Alberta Canby.

UNL Omaha language class posing with the shawls they made. Seated in the center of the front row are Native speakers Emmaline Sanchez and Alberta Canby.

Omaha language speaker Emmaline Sanchez and University of Nebraska anthropology professor Mark Awakuni-Swetland honoring remnants of the old Omaha dance lodges.

Clan markers, Omaha tribal council building, Macy. The clan markers follow the circular form of the building.

Clan marker, Omaha tribal council building. Elder and Native speaker
Alberta Canby in the background.

Marker for Alice Saunsoci's clan, the Thátada, in the Omaha tribal council building, Macy.

Marker for Alice Saunsoci's clan, the Close-up of Alice Saunsoci's clan marker.

Clan marker, Omaha tribal council building.

3. Eleanor Baxter

Tribal Chair and Political Activist

I was born about three miles west of here, in a house out in
the country—a house that didn't have electricity, no running
water, no inside toilet, and none of the conveniences. And I
can remember going up there and our only way to get anywhere was to walk or ride a wagon with horses pulling it. That
was our transportation. The rest of the time, we walked. It
wasn't unusual to see people walking whenever they wanted
to go to the nearest town, Walthill, which was three miles
from us. And then Macy is another three miles. And we were
right in between and used to walking.

I was born in that house where my life began and because
there were no housing units at that time, in the summertime,
we would sleep outside. My brother would spread a canvas on
the ground, and back in those days, there wasn't transportation, so we were quite safe sleeping in front of the porch. And

Eleanor Baxter

my mother would lay the canvas down and sleep with my dad and all the kids. We would spread out on that canvas—it was just a way of living that was accepted.

Our neighbors across the street had a black and white TV, and sometimes they would let us watch it. It was such a treat to go across and watch black and white TV. It opened up a different world for us, and we used to all sit there and wish we could have TV.

We lived with my grandparents, Minnie Furnace Turner was her maiden name. She was the daughter of Zhiⁿgágahi, which meant "Little Chief." Her father lived to be 115 years old. She married Frank Saunsoci, who was my grandfather. He was born in the 1880s. My grandmother was born in the 1880s. They married and from his first marriage, my grandfather had eight children. I don't quite know the story of the marriage to my grandmother but he had eight children, of which my father came from. The only one I knew from there was my aunt, Elizabeth Stabler. She and my dad were full brother and sister. My dad was just a young man when my grandfather passed away. He was born in 1912. In 1917, he lost his own father.

My grandmother had another family. In the process she lost six children. I never knew that. I don't even know how she lost the six children, but I would say my grandfather Frank was quite the man, having seventeen children. I'm always amazed! We were told there were some Saunsoci women who had left and had never returned to the reservation. They went with the Mormon Church and migrated. We understand that we may have relatives living in Canada, and we have met some people out on the West Coast who have corresponded with us, but they wanted to trace their heritage from Lewis Saunsoci, who was an interpreter for the Omaha tribe. We have some relationship with the ones I met in Idaho, so that part of life is interesting too.

My grandmother, Minnie, remarried the man I call "Grandpa," whose name was Harry Solomon. He was a tall, thin man and wore long braids and couldn't speak very good English. My grandmother did all the English. They had two children, Joe Solomon and Georgine Solomon. So my dad had an addition of a sister and a brother. They continued their life together in that house out west where I was born.

My mother was an orphan. She and my father found each other. She married at a real young age, eighteen, and I was one of eleven children. I'm the second oldest of the Saunsoci women. How they did it back in those days is beyond me. She spaced her children every two years and breast fed every one of us. And I can look at her as having no help. And having no support system because she, herself, lost her mother when she was six or seven of quick consumption.

My grandmother divorced my grandfather. His name was Hiram Blackbird. The relationship wasn't working. She remarried another man that my mother became quite fond of because he was so good to her and her brothers. (My mother had three brothers—Blackbirds. I still have their marriage certificate.) My grandmother's original name was Maggie Morris, and when she married she was Maggie Morris Blackbird. Then she divorced him and took the name of Kemp. Some of these names were taken from the missionaries, from church people, the church denominations who used to come to the reservation. The Mormons. There were several different churches that used to come here. The Catholics. I couldn't tell you how many churches came through here, but they all tried to convert Indians to Christianity. That's how the names came to be. Before that, there were clan names. The Omahas have ten clans and seven tribal seats on the tribal council. But we didn't have clanship because of my father. My grandmother had a clan name. I do know that my mother was from the Mo^{n}thí^{n}kagaxe clan. She was from the Earth People. And I do know that my grandmother was Hó^{n}ga. My great-great-grandfather, his name was Yellow Smoke. She (my grandmother) was the daughter of Yellow Smoke. When I found that out, I was quite amazed because my mother never talked about that. There was a picture of him. Yellow Smoke had four children. He had one named Cora, my grandmother, Maggie, and he had Carrie. Then they had a son named Tom. We used to call him Grandpa Tom Smoke because he was the son of Yellow Smoke. I remember him. He didn't have any children. They lost their sister, Maggie, my grandmother, to quick consumption. The care of the Blackbird children was left to Carrie, who was a Drum by then—Carrie Drum. She raised my mother and two of the brothers. She had many children—I would say seven or eight. Today, they're all deceased. I'm thankful that my grandma took my mother in and raised her. They lived in a house south of here.

My mother met my dad when he was nineteen. He was a singer in the Native American Church. He could sing Indian songs. They made their life together and out of that marriage came eleven of us children. There was my brother, Oliver, the oldest. Oliver was raised by my Grandma and Grandpa Soloman. Back then, it was normal and a custom to take the oldest grandchild and to raise them. My oldest daughter, Yolanda, was raised by her grandparents. We were living in Lincoln and they were planning to move back to Macy in 1973, to return home. He told me, "Get her ready and I'm going to take your oldest one and raise her as my own." I had no choice. You did not sass your folks. So that's how that happened. In 1973, my dad decided that he should return back to Macy. It was time for him to come home. He was in his sixties then. My mother followed my dad, although she didn't want to leave Lincoln because all of us—her children were there. But she came back with my dad.

I was seven when we moved to Lincoln. That was my home so I got to know about life here. In Lincoln, we never forgot the language or the customs. We never forgot that we came from the Omaha tribe. But we were educated in Lincoln among a multicultural society. It was easy because I was always one to be on top. I was never one to sit back and be real quiet. There were eleven of us, and Oliver was the oldest. He joined the military at seventeen to fight a war—the Korean

War. And he came back and survived it. Never talked about any of the war, what happened over there. Kept it to himself and sometimes I always think that when people fight in wars, that they really could use some counseling. But that didn't happen. And he probably went out to sweat and to the hills to pray. That's what we used to do. That's what used to happen. People go out into the wilderness and sit on a hill and pray and think. And then there was Mary Ann. She was next and was my companion. She died four years ago in November. She was everything to me—my teacher, my mentor, my mother. There was ten years between us. I still miss her today. I would go sit by her grave. Then I would cry for her. One morning, I would say at four o'clock, I was just laying there thinking about her because I was still grieving really bad for her. And all of a sudden this loud voice came out and said, "Eleanor!" and I said, "Mary Ann!" She made her voice known to me and that voice was happy and strong. And I knew that she was okay. From that day on, it was a sign to me to quit, to quit! I was happy. I laid in bed and I smiled when I heard her voice. And I really believe that and I haven't cried for her since. Knowing that she didn't have to suffer and knowing that she was good. And then I have Frank. He died four months after Mary Ann did. That's Alice's husband. In between, my mother had some children I never knew—a brother and sister. Annabelle. I didn't know her. And Henry. Then came my brother Charlie. He just passed in August. To me, he's still in Lincoln because you know, I never saw him that much and I always tried to call him and sometimes I'd get a hold of him and sometimes I wouldn't. He died in August and that left me. I had a sister name Rhea who was hit by a car at seven and she died. After that, there was my sister Maxine who still resides in Lincoln. More than likely, she will never come home. Lincoln is her home and she has a house right there.

They own their home and her children, one's going to Wayne State and the other one is at UNL. Then my sister Cora, she lives here in Macy. I had a younger brother, Vince, who passed away. They're all buried up here in Macy cemetery, right beside each other. So, that's the happy hunting grounds.

I keep going because I have to. I have children to look after and I am their mentor. They come to me when they are in need of someone to talk to and I'm the kind of person, if they're doing something wrong, I'll tell them. Because I care. And they know that. I'm not afraid to say I said it. They will tell me, You can't keep a secret, mom." Moms can keep a secret, but then I have to tell them. That's my job. If I was to keep secrets, I'd have so many to carry around that I wouldn't be a good mother. So if anything happens to my children, I have to tell them.

I have Yolanda, who is going to be thirty-four in May. Shannon is thirty-two. My son is twenty. His name is Everett Junior. He's at United Tribe and will graduate soon. I wanted him to go to an Indian school to meet other tribes. I told him, "One day you will meet some successful young Indian people, and when you get to school, they might say, 'Come work for me.'" I want all of my children to have an education. That is the key. The girls have their associates degree, which is a start. I don't want them to struggle for jobs. My only way out of this was to finish high school, and I did that in Lincoln,

I lived with my mom, Mae Blackbird Saunsoci, and my dad, Oliver Saunsoci Senior. We lived in an apartment in

Lincoln, right on O Streets, 1821 O. My first school was El-liot. I grew up in West Lincoln where the Phillips Manor is. Right on the corner. We grew up there. That shouldn't be the Phillips Manor—it should be the Saunsoci Manor be-cause we grew up there. That was before the Interstate was built. That whole road down there used to be a dirt road. The Hudsons—they were the biggest people in the Belmont area. They owned the Hudson's Store. There was a hog farm right in the back, on 4th and Adams Street, near Gaslight Village where the trailer camp is.

That was before all the trailers moved in, but that was where we grew up and we used to walk from 4th all the way to West Lincoln, every day. We all teamed up, all of us neighborhood kids. We were friends with a family that used to have goats. And there was a black family. We used to go off to school to-gether. We went to a country school then. I could have grad-uated from eighth grade (at the country school) but the city decided to incorporate and take us in. Then it changed. I could take the bus and go to Whittier in the ninth grade. I graduated from Whittier and met a whole new combination of people there.

My dad worked for Abel Construction and my mother worked for Capitol Hotel. She was a dishwasher and salad maker. They worked long hours! In those days, they didn't have any vocation programs. My mother went to eighth grade and graduated from Genoa Indian School. She was consid-ered to be educated. I took her back there in 1963. At that time, the buildings were still standing—the school and all the buildings. There were scorched windows and empty . . . but it was still there. It was a military type boot camp. She has fond memories of Genoa. Because it was military style, they all had to wear their hair like in "Nancy and Sluggo cartoons."

They wore uniforms and they had bugle call in the morning to get them up. She stayed until eighth grade and graduated, then went back to live with Grandma Carrie in Macy. There was no work here. No houses. Everyone lived in tents. You should have seen it. Nothing but shanties. Yeah, shanties. There was no inside toilet. Everybody had an outside toilet and everybody got their water down here, south of the school [*Umóⁿhoⁿ Nation Public School*]. There was a tank. And water from underground wells. Or at the church. We used to draw spring water from wells west of Macy using milk cans and buckets. Even the outside water from that came from the springs.

Everybody prepared for the winter to come. Cutting wood. My grandparents used to grow big gardens and can. And prepare for the winter—canning tomatoes and beans and corn—blue corn. It was used for hominy or for mush, corn mush. And sweetener added to make it sweet. We used to pick gooseberries and raspberries. We weren't afraid of snakes or anything. Lots of times, we would go barefooted because we didn't have shoes to wear. We were so poor and yet we didn't realize it. I knew every inch of that countryside, going through the woods. In the wintertime, we used to go sledding. That was our entertainment. There was a hill.

My mother worked for Harper-Smith when it came into being. She worked for Abel Hall. She was tiny and cute—a great mom. Never drank or smoked. Just a good mom. No beer, cigarettes. Anything. Hard-working woman. She told all of us, "You go to school. You go and get a decent job." I came right through that era where the civil rights movement . . . 1963, when Martin Luther was speaking, when the American Indian Movement and Cesar Chavez came out. I grew up in that era. That's when Rosa Parks rode that bus. Indian people were barely recognized. We had to fight our way. We were called savages, dirty Indians. We were called names. But we were kids so we fought back. We said the same thing with words. You know, you're kids so you don't care and we pushed each other and actually got into fights. The name-calling is stereotypical. We'd tell the white kids we were fighting, "You guys should jump on the Mayflower and go back across the ocean." We'd throw it back. It was nothing. We'd see each other and we'd go at it. That's the way life was.

I had some good teachers in Lincoln. Guidance teachers didn't know how to deal with Indians. Lots of people couldn't handle Indian people because they didn't know what kind of people we were. Sometimes, you could see that they really didn't know how to handle you. Why that was, I don't know, because I was one of the few people that wasn't really bashful. He [one of the guidance counselors] was good to the rich kids. Lincoln rich kids went to Lincoln High School. I made myself join clubs—Stenographer's Club. And I was in Pep Club. And there were several other clubs that I was in, but you know, I wanted to make it in the school. I've always been one of those people who tried to make it.

After high school, I worked at Miller & Paine on 13th and O Street, making their cinnamon rolls and bread. That was my young life. I was nineteen. I knew my life wouldn't be the bakery, but it helped pay the bills. I wanted to help my folks. And then I thought, no, this isn't for me after working at those ovens for a year. One summer I was just sweating, sweating. And the windows were open, clear up on the ninth floor.

I knew it wasn't the bakery. It was a job and helped pay the bills. I wanted to help my folks. Then right next door to us was a candy place where they made chocolate. One day, I went to Ben's, the hairdresser. I went over there and said, "I've got the tuition." My mom paid the tuition. I was a hairdresser for sixteen years. Loved it! I worked in Havelock (in north Lincoln) for five years for JaRee Beauty Salon. I worked there—the only Indian. I knew everybody in Havelock. Then I went downtown and managed Clip and Curl. I managed another place on 27th and O Street—kept the books and mailed in quarterly reports to the state. I never thought of coming back to Macy in those days! I met my husband in Lincoln. He's from here. We knew each other growing up.

I worked for the Lincoln Action Program for seven years and learned to help the Human Services. Then I went back to school at Southeast Community College. I was there in 1987. In 1990, after working for LAP, I got the Woman of Color Award. It was just something that I did normally, but I was recognized for it. I won a national award from the Job Training Partnership Act as an outstanding achiever. They recognized me in Milwaukee. Alice Roach of the JTPA saw that I achieved and could work anywhere because I could just talk. The thing you have to do is have communication skills. It'll get you far. The late Alice Roach was the JTPA director at the Lincoln Indian Center. When they took me to Milwaukee to accept the award, I was a little bit timid when I got up there to make a speech. I could always talk, but at the time, I didn't know how to talk to the public. I could talk privately, like this. And today, it's totally different. I can get up in front of an organization, a group and talk and know my facts. That's what it takes. Good eye contact. In our custom, you don't look directly into the eyes.

My husband wanted to come back to Macy. I didn't want to. I was comfortable in my house. I loved my house. I loved when it rained and I could look outside from my bedroom. It was on 1305 North 21st Street, right down from that little filling station going over the bridge on Holdrege. I had two rooms in the attic, four rooms upstairs, a bathroom and downstairs, a huge living room and a breakfast nook and dining area and downstairs a huge basement. I didn't want to leave that when I came home to a trailer out in Onawa, Iowa, which is about twenty-five miles from Macy. There were no houses to be found. My husband was working. I wasn't even looking for a job. I was really unsettled being here because I didn't want to be. I felt really bad for leaving Lincoln. My kids were already here. My daughter, Yolanda, grew up here.

I wasn't looking for a job when we returned to Macy in 1993. We had to have rent money and grocery money, deposits for lights and gas, had to fix our car and pay car insurance. I had ten dollars. I went to the casino and thought, well, I'm going to gamble this ten dollars, and I got ten silver dollars. I stuck two in the dollar machine and then I was going to go down to five and save the rest for gas. But on the second spin, I hit the jackpot and it was worth two thousand dollars! I was just screaming and screaming! We really needed that money. Someone must have been looking out for us. Then one day, the snow was falling. Blizzard conditions. It was a Friday night. I saw this application for case manager for Healthy Start—for pregnant women. I applied for it. The deadline was at 4:30 and it was just 4:30. I turned it in and lo and behold, I got a letter saying I got an interview. I went for that and got hired. It was at the Carl T. Curtis Clinic. They sent me to training in Aberdeen, South Dakota. I worked there for five years. Never paid any attention to tribal politics. Could have cared less about it because I liked my job. I liked helping and knew all about pregnancies and just educated myself. Then there was a director position for the JTPA, the employment and training program. I applied for that and got an interview and was hired! All my life, I have never had to worry about jobs. Jobs just came to me, even in the city. I stayed at my jobs because I liked them. With the JTPA, I had to write my own contracts and learn how to do budgets. I went all over for training—to California, Texas, Minnesota. I had that job from 1997 to October 2001. Then one day, my girls, husband, Ida Blackbird, and my niece, Adrianna said, "Mom, we paid for your filing fee of thirty dollars and you're ready for tribal council. You're gonna make it. Because people like you." And I said, "Oh—what did you do!" They said, "Well, we already got the petition." Yeah, you have to have twenty-five registered voters. They did all my forms for me. But I didn't want to get into tribal politics. I knew nothing about tribal politics. I got elected, sworn in. I was just one nervous wreck! I didn't know what I was getting myself into because I had to learn . . . didn't know anything about the constitution. I knew nothing. I never paid attention to tribal politics. I figured other people—councilmen, council people, were running our reservation. I was elected in for three years. It has an orientation process of three years. I had to learn about the Bureau [*the Bureau of Indian Affairs*] and programs, the law enforcement, Head Start program, all the programs. Before you know it, my three years are up and there comes the 2004 elections. I still was in the top. We went to staggered terms—three, two, and one. So there would be consistency. This means the ones with the highest votes got three years—three of them got three years. The next got two and one—in consecutive order. I got the third highest vote which shows that people have confidence in me. On November second, I took office again for three more years as vice chair. Today, I have enough confidence. I still need help in some areas. But most of the time, I like to talk so I know the issues at hand and can conduct business. It's a lot of hard work and responsibility and I always think I just want to go ahead and retire. But I'll see how I'm feeling after three years. If I want to try it for two or one more term. Then that will take me right up to age sixty-five or sixty-six.

What I love most about tribal politics is that it's challenging. So many challenges among our people. We're described by the media as high-poverty areas, stricken high-poverty areas. The terminology they use on us is unfair because we have to live with what we have. If President Bush was looking out for people of the country, he would give us more money for programs, for job opportunities. I disagree with his policymaking. He needs to clean up his own backyard before he pours billions into a country that should be helping themselves. When we go to Washington, we have to fight for what we have. We shouldn't have to fight. This was our land! It was our land! And I'm real passionate about our land. Those are the kinds of things we have to fight for.

We have several programs that are going. We're going to have to have a big meeting to focus on drugs and get our law enforcement people to see how many drug arrests have been made and see who's using. People talk. Kids talk. Did you know so and so's on drugs and I'm not. They are? My own family's using drugs. They're into it. The meth. They're into it. And it's ruining them. They don't want to give it up. They're hooked. And I feel sorry for them. I can't help them because words don't help. My brothers can't even talk to them because their minds have been made up. Yeah, so that's how I stumbled into tribal politics.

I go all over—to Aberdeen, to Omaha for judicial or coalition meetings. And it's nothing for us to go to Lincoln. We're going to some different conferences out of state. California is nothing anymore. Utah, Phoenix, Las Vegas. We go. We meet with all the Indian nations—the National Congress of the American Indians.

So this is where I grew up. This is where I was born. Me and my sister and my two brothers were born here and an old German family used to live here. We got all their milk and eggs. This white house here (across the road, northwest from Eleanor's home) was the school that used to sit uphill over there. This is where I went to school when it was sitting up there.

There was a vine down here that we'd swing off of. There'd be two or three of us and there used to be a little bit of water in there. Not much of a creek, but enough to get your feet wet. And we'd follow that all the way down to where I told you we picked gooseberries. It's spring water. Yeah, oh yeah, we used to take an old hood right here, down the first hill. When it snowed so much, we'd take an old hood and we would slick it down. We had several places where we took hoods. We had so much energy. We were kids! And my brothers knew how to make bobsleds. They would slick them up. We'd go sledding in the nighttime, after our eyes got used to the dark. We weren't afraid of coyotes or anything. There used to be a waterway down here. These houses weren't there.

This was the hill where we used to go way fast. We'd make my dad go real fast and we would just laugh because it took our breath away. But yeah. That was our hill where it took our stomachs away. I had to do that for you.

Now we're fighting for issues or fighting for better housing. Health care issues. Health care is the number one priority because we have diabetes so rampant. And cancer has become so widespread. A year ago in November, I'm a cancer survivor. I had endometrial cancer. So I'm a survivor of that and I thank the Lord for letting me see my children. When I look all around me, there are younger people dying and for some reason, maybe, He saw that my work was important and He spared my life and I thank Him every day for that.

My grandmother wore the Mark of Honor. She was a medicine woman. But we've lost many of our healers. The women. I'm sorry to say that none of us, she didn't take one of us aside to say, "I'm going to teach you." We used to go to healing ceremonies and she would know where the trees and the plants . . . to cut the herbs for healing. And everything for the toothache. And there was a certain kind of root that she gathered and I remember her mixing them in bowls. But when she went into her healing ceremonies, we weren't allowed. So, it was something you had to earn. But somehow, she didn't teach us.

[*While we were driving the countryside, Big Elk Park came into view—a winding dirt road bordered by massive cottonwoods and deciduous trees. The road led to the Missouri River.*]

This is our river landing. It goes all the way back. And we're going to put in a dredge, to reopen the Hole in the Rock. It's just the name for the road going down, and when you come to it, the edges of it, they're rock plates. There's names dating back, names written on there.

They're going to refill the Missouri—stock it up. So many lives were lost in that river. That's why the swimming pool was built because kids were coming down her to the river to swim and the current's too strong. And the deer are so plentiful here. White tails. Used to be a house back here too.

[*We drove to another dirt road, edged by thickets of raspberry bushes. Debris from another house lay near these thickets. Eleanor told me how a long time ago, a woman was shot by her boyfriend in this area and was left there for several nights.*]

It was in March. I'm surprised she didn't die then. But she said what kept her alive were those little people. We talk about little people here. They're visible to some. She said they were giving her water and they kept her going.

[*We entered Macy from Big Elk Park. Eleanor told me about the road called Million Dollar Hill that led from the northeast into town, dug with shovels during the era of the* WPA *in the thirties. On either side rose high dirt hills. She explained that manpower created the phenomenon of the bluffs and road.*]

They dug it out by shovel. It was clear over here—all the way down. You can envision the land base here. [*She showed me where she lived, east of the tribal council building.*] My rocks, you see my rocks. Look at my flowers growing already—irises and tulips. Everybody is always used to seeing us outside, cleaning our yard. Because we have to keep it clean. My husband keeps a good yard. This is where we live.

[*The next time I saw Eleanor, it was to clarify any transcription mistakes. Two months had passed. I met her and Alice Saunsoci in Eleanor's office. She was visibly upset by the portrayal of In-dians in the media.*]

I told Wynne I would take some time. Alice Saunsoci is here and I'm going to be having a meeting. I asked her the ques-tion, "The first thing that you hear from the media—what do you hear?" She mentioned White Clay, the article in the *Lincoln Journal Star* newspaper, the Sunday issue of May 15, 2005. [*White Clay is a town located in Nebraska directly south of the Pine Ridge Indian reservation, right across the border.*] The real answer is what you hear in the media about Indian nations—the high rate of unemployed people and the impov-erished nation is how Indian people are usually described by the media. When you look at Indian people, that's what they look at. And when you look at Congress and all its legislation, where do they earmark dollars for programs for Indians? You don't see that. And in the budget, you don't see the increases. Where does that money go? It goes all over, internationally, into the international countries where impoverished nations are. Our government does not look in their own backyard and see . . . I get highly upset about that.

Because with our minds and with our dollars, we didn't have the sustainability to pick up on this. We didn't realize that there were tax credits, tax dollars around. Those things are new to us. Aside from that, look at our banks. Look at how we didn't have the employment. How could we get a bank loan? How could we guarantee that bank loan that should be paid? That's the only way you can get some of these bonds is if you're a tribe, then you can use the tribe's name and there is income from land leases, there's income from direct ser-vice costs and through taxes and those kinds of things. But you know, I've looked at this long and hard—that progress is very slow in coming, and one day, we hope to be flourishing with that economy.

Alcohol is always number one. They don't look at the good people. They use alcohol in comparison to the tradition and the culture, the goodness of our people. We are not selfish with how we live—we share. We don't have . . . if we don't have the money, we find other ways of contributing to our reservation that we live in. And we all know that. We can walk around without a dollar, we can especially! Money comes hard for us. But yet, when we do get those dollars, who do we contribute to? The economy of South Sioux City, of Sioux City generally.

Do you see department stores here? We don't have that. Do you see a grocery store? We have a convenience store. But yeah, that's for gas and for conveniences. It has bread, lunchmeat, chips, candy, and pop. But it's not big enough for a grocery store. We are looking along the lines of having that and those things are going to happen, with time, and they are in the planning. When you plan, it doesn't happen overnight. We're slowly becoming business oriented so that we can think better about how we can keep those dollars into our economy here. And provide employment. We have long-range thinking, but we have to think about how we're going to maintain such things as a strip mall. How are we going to get people in there that are going to know about plans—business plans. Inventory? How to fill out taxes for the state of Nebraska. There's planning, planning, planning. Learning, learning, learning. It's going to happen one day. As our people get educated, I think those things could happen quicker.

[*Eleanor went on to talk about the money from Macy going to department stores such as JCPenney, Sears, and Foot Locker, about how she went to these stores to ask for donations.*]

I was told I'd have to wait until the next funding cycle. It's upsetting when you are told that, knowing that these are big, big stores. Big multimillion dollar stores that are making the money from all four of the tribes here in Nebraska—Ponca, Winnebago, Santee Sioux, and us. And when you ask for a contribution and get a twenty-five or fifty dollar contribution. Sure! It's money. But come on! When you read the paper and they're contributing ten thousand, fifteen, twenty to other nations. I don't think that's right. We know that in rural America we're not the only ones. There are over 550 nations and we all have problems with, number one, employment. I would say economic development would be the hardest. Ideas go in my head as to how we can get those big company contracts and put our people to work. There's so many things that are going on in this world that we should be a part of and we're being left out. Probably because we don't know how to go about it. But we're thinking along those lines. We hope to be—it's a big goal for self-sufficiency, for the state, for Nebraska.

[*Alice Saunsoci agreed. She took the microphone and said if they are going to reach self-sufficiency certain things would have to happen. She talked about how the monthly checks handicapped their people and how they had become dependent.*]

We're only one tribe. Civilized as they call us about a hundred and fifty years ago. And we're still learning. We have all got to learn. Our children, our young people are being prepared slowly. When your culture, when you have a child, you think about college, you put money away for college or a home. But we're still down here. Still struggling to survive with our children, with ourselves, combating what Eleanor said is alcoholism that was brought here. And there was a purpose for that. It was a form of killing us off. So when they said they couldn't kill us people, then that's okay. They can kill themselves with the alcohol. I worked hard all my life. We just survived. We didn't have much money in the bank. We did something for our children when they were in high school at graduation. And then, after they reached the high school graduation, we came here to live in Macy. You mentioned why our monies are going into the city. There's no money coming here. There isn't anything here to spend our money on. We have to leave. Thirty, forty miles away, we've got to go. So with us, it's a way to get away sometimes, if you want to be away from home, but it costs us money. We're not keeping our money here. The other thing is with our education. When they go specialize to be an accountant or to be anything, and when you finish, if there's a job waiting for us. We have to think about those things. Our young people are becoming aware. They're wanting to go to school and get their education. Some go to higher education, some go to UNL, Omaha, (UNO) Creighton—wherever they want to go. There again, they haven't been prepared.

[*Alice turned to Eleanor and they talked about a workshop to prepare their young people for college, for the rigors of studying and job search skills, and how to find a place to live while they are going to school. I asked both Alice and Eleanor how they saw themselves as role models for the younger generation. Alice spoke first.*]

Well, we want the economy and the business they bring in, but we also—my role I see as an elder is to change, mostly revitalize, our language. That's what I'm into. I'm very big on our language so our children can learn, so they can go off to school and become linguists, whatever. Come back and be teachers because we have a public school down here.

But they don't have anything about our culture. There is no Native American Studies here. Like the tribal government. How our tribal council and government operates. And the Umóⁿhoⁿ—there is much to learn. To know who we are. Some of our kids, they don't know that. We're working on that. Bringing in Umóⁿhoⁿ history at the school.

[*Eleanor said that the Omaha tribe land base is 31,148 acres. Of the original land base of 300,000 acres awarded, that is what is left.*][1]

There were no laws to protect the sale of that land, and even Blackbird Hill is not owned by the tribe. It's owned by non-Indians. We're going to appeal it. That's part of our history.

[*Eleanor, Alice, and I talked longer about the future of the tribe, about how Indian people are being "forceful for their causes." Eleanor's son is headed to the University of Nebraska in Lincoln after graduating from United Tribes Technical College in Bismarck, North Dakota. She wants him to learn, then come home. But first, she wants him to be mainstreamed, to live multiculturally because then he can talk on anybody's level.*]

I greet every day with a good morning and a prayer. To get me through the day. And ask the Creator for the strength to do my job and to watch over our people. And all of our people in a foreign country. Pray for just the things that normally go on in our routine. I seek help for our people—always for the health care, for all the tragedies that we have suffered and now the social ills, the drug scenes.

[*Eleanor went to a meeting and Alice said she would drive me around her corner of the reservation where she grew up. As we walked to the car, I glanced back at the council building. Inside, I was sure, things were changing.*]

4. Alice Saunsoci

Language Bearer and Teacher

My name is Alice Fern Fremont Saunsoci, Umóⁿhoⁿ izházhe wiwíta Móⁿshi [*"My Omaha name is Moⁿshi"*]. I was born November 25, 1937. I lived between Macy and Decatur. I was raised by my grandparents, Emma Parker Kemp and John Horse Kemp. I was not raised by my parents. As a child, I lived out there in the rural area, as we call it today. My grandparents were farmers. They farmed, they raised their own garden. They had horses. We had chickens and hogs. No cows. And our duties were to help take care of the animals. I remember that. We had a dog, a cat. What I remember . . . my grandmother did not speak English. She was very traditional. She spoke nothing but Omaha language. My grandfather, John, he attended Carlisle [*Carlisle Indian School*]—that's where he went to school. So he knew English. And he translated a lot for my grandmother. We did not go to school early on. She

Alice Saunsoci

was very suspicious or she didn't really trust the white people. There were times that this lady came to our place where I was raised and when this white lady would show up, my grandmother would say, "Go inside. This bad white woman has come." And so, we went inside and she would call for my grandfather and tell him, "Go over there and speak to her." And she directed my grandfather to do this. He would talk to this lady out on the road and when he came back, we said, "What did she want? What did that white woman want?" I must've been school age then—about five. And I'd ask him, "Waxe wa?ú iⁿdádoⁿ góⁿtha?" What did that white woman want? And he would say, "Well, she is the superintendent of the county." I had no idea what the "superintendent" did in those days. But she was the one that always came. She never did come into the house or yard. The conversation was out on the road, so he spoke to her out on the road and it was always the same—wondering why we weren't in school.

When I was nine I attended McCauley School [*a one-room school about six miles south of Macy*]. It's still standing. My grandmother passed away and my grandfather one day said that I was to attend school. But in the meantime, our grandparents raised some other children. I wasn't the only one. They were, I guess, to the modern-day term now, considered foster parents. One of the orphan boys taught me how to write my name, know my numbers, my ABC's. But Omaha language was spoken in my home. That's my first language. According to my grandfather, he said I was to go to school, and we didn't live very far from there, maybe a quarter of a mile. He walked me to school. He came, took me in. I went in the schoolroom, schoolhouse, and there was a desk. He had everything in front of the desk—all the school supplies. Everything was there. The teacher and I used gestures. I pointed at the things I wanted, but the one that caught my eye was this tablet. It was red and it had a chief on it. Indian. To me, that was beautiful. I picked that out first. And I went down the line to get all the school supplies I wanted. Then he showed me where I was to sit, pulled the chair around. I sat there. And my grandfather left. He said for me to stay there, he was leaving. So I stayed.

I had never set foot in that class [*until that day*]. The teacher, Mr. Conklin, explained some things to me. I looked at everybody. There were other children there. We had white kids, Indian kids. I looked at them, they looked at me. We all looked at each other and I sat down. He gave me a book, a "Dick and Jane" book by the way.

There was a young lady in eighth grade—she was getting ready to graduate. We continued this gesturing and he would read the book to me and point at the pictures. As the years went by, I realized that my grandfather must have told him I couldn't speak English. He was very understanding. And so I learned how to read. Other things he didn't have to teach me because I already knew how to write my name. I knew my ABC's and my numbers. I knew my counting by twos, fives, tens, and my times tables. The way I learned this—my cousin came home. It must have been Christmas. He brought me a present. This chalkboard, some chalks. It had an easel. He set it up and taught me. I thank him today. His name was Clifford Hallowell. He's now deceased. He lived with us. Like I said, there were a lot of us. He taught me those so with that, I had no trouble. He must have gone off to school somewhere because he could do blueprints. I don't know what you call them today. That was his job. He designed elevators.

My grandmother taught us to be respectful people. She taught us our behavior, our role as ladies, growing up ladies. One of them was, if there were let's say, two, three men standing over here [*she stood and walked to the side of her chair*] and we're heading toward them, even before we get there we say, "Shubthé-tami^{n}k^{h}e," and then we would either move all the way this way or they would move like this. [*She wrapped her skirt close to her legs so the material didn't touch anything.*] When we went by, no part of our clothing touched them. That's how we went. We went around them. We never went between them or in front of them. And that still stands today. But they do it differently if some lady my age was going down this street and this man standing over there where she's going, she's going to go around. That's still there. We still have this in a different manner. So she spoke of Wakónda, God, to us—to pray. She also taught me to cook, to plant gardens. When we planted gardens, we would go out there and pray. We do not allow small children to come and plant our food. The reasoning is the crops are going to be small. Those are some of the beliefs she had. When everything was up and going good, then we went out there to—guess what? Pull weeds! Hoe the garden. We helped take care of it. I'm of the Thátada clan and some of our cousins were not that clan.[1] Certain clans cannot go out and garden. Certain clans cannot go out and name the date for powwow or anything. That was our belief that my grandfather, grandmother taught us—that certain clans can't come into the garden or tend to it. They could do other things that were helpful and, you know, get hot water, help prepare foods and other things, but they couldn't go off and actually do what we did. That was one of the teachings that we had.

My grandmother did her grocery shopping in Decatur and Lyons.[2] When we went to Lyons, she spoke of the proprietor as *síthede bazu*.[3] They spoke in Umónhon, carried on this conversation. He tells her what's going on in Lyons, she tells him what's going on here on our reservation. And they carried this on and she ordered everything in our language and he got it. He gave them to her. Today, it's not so. You don't see that. He was white, but he knew the Omaha language. Back in those days, they had to. That was their survival because they had to learn to speak our language if they owned stores and other businesses. *Síthede bazu* is talking about the heel. He wore an orthopedic shoe. Part of one shoe was higher than the other. He was a handicapped person. He wore that kind of shoe. That's where she did her grocery

shopping, and clothing probably. You could go in one place
and just buy everything. Walmart. See, Walmart is like these
stores way back when. But we had our own apple orchard.
We had our chokecherry bush. We had a strawberry patch.
And the farmer going toward, between Lyons and Decatur,
he had orchards. Pears. Some peaches. We had two, three
pear trees that belonged to us. The other two trees belonged
to the Parkers. And then the other was his. We picked them,
took them home, and canned them. My grandmother did a
lot of canning. And we butchered. We never went to the grocery store to buy meat. She would tell my grandfather, "Téska
tanúka bthátʰe kóⁿbtha," I'm hungry for beef.[4] He'd go and
bring that beef home. They would say their prayers and everything, have their rituals, then would shoot the animal. We
laid it down and went in and they would shoot it. And it's all
fine. So when they bring the meat, everything, they're haul-
ing it and here we are. Kids. We did the pumping because
there was constant water coming. They washed it. Everything.
Rinsed the meat. Once they did all that, they put salt on it.
Cooking salt? Tanning salt? We didn't have a smokehouse.
They used salt and we had a porch that had a roof. They had
small logs that were crossed and the meat was there. We had
this window and we'd open that and fall out there and go
get what meat we wanted and take it down. That was what
we did. She also fried the meat, roasted it. And she canned it.
Canned that fried meat, pork chops, whatever. She canned it
and you know, it never spoiled.

[*The annual tribal buffalo hunt of the Omaha took place during the summer. The entire tribe participated with great cere-
mony; it was called* té úne *(Té means "buffalo"; úne means "to
seek" or "to look for") and took place after the cultivation of the*

corn. *The winter hunt was called* Máthe té úne *and was done to secure pelts. Since the principal supply of meat and pelts were secured through these hunts, it was important to honor the buffalo with appropriate ceremonies and prayers. The religious rites recognized the power and dependence of Wakǒⁿda, but also recognized the importance of ceremonial observance by the people. When the animals were butchered, their flesh bore a common name,* tá, *when dried. When fresh, it was referred to as* tanúka, *or fresh meat (see Fletcher and La Flesche 270-71). Ritual prayers, in Alice's world as a young girl, were ongoing and vital cultural traditions framed her stories.*]

She canned everything. The meat, whatever else that was edible. We had a lot of dried food. She canned milkweeds. Dried mushrooms. When winter came, we didn't have any microwave ovens back in those days, but you know, we had the wood stove. She warmed everything up—opened the meat and warmed it up. I remember one time that a blizzard, the snow was blowing as it was in those days. We were eating milkweed soup. It was already boiled or however they prepared it. We had that. The mushrooms were dried. And she put them away nice. Then fixed them. Put them in water and they came back to almost their natural form. Fried them. So that's what she did. Canned everything. Dried meat. I must have been about seven or eight when I learned to dry meat. I was the one that helped her and the one that lay out the clothesline. She had a long clothesline and she'd be out there with a rag to clean that wire up really good. And we'd take that meat. And there again, she sprinkled it with salt. It'd be out there drying and my thing was, I had to keep the birds and flies away. She'd check the meat and then add salt. If it's not that dry, next day we'd be back at it. Drying. Once she was satisfied with it, she packed it away. And all of a sudden she would get that meat out and clean it up real good, boil it, put potatoes in there. But what I remember is the squash. She sliced it. I helped her do it. We bought it in quantities when we went grocery shopping. She always bought the syrup in big cans and the coffee in bags. Columbia coffee. She bought that. And that was my job again. She roasted the coffee herself the way she wanted it and then she'd give me some. I took it and put it in this little square coffee grinder. A wooden one. Put it in there and ground it four, five, six turns. I showed it to her and she would take it and see if the grounds were the way she wanted it.

[*The Omaha's adaptation to the reservation was described as "remarkable." In the fall of 1850, Agent John Robertson noted that they raised six thousand bushels of corn on the 125-acre government field and in their own fields. They had successful winter and summer buffalo hunts in 1856-57 that brought in eight hundred robes, skins, "and large amounts of bison and deer meat" (Wishart 121). Farming efforts were intensified owing to the realization that buffalo and deer meat would soon be scarce. In 1861, they produced twenty thousand bushels of corn. Population increases, due to abundant food, reached 950 in 1861—450 males and 500 females (121). This was a stark contrast to the prereservation era when the Dakota drove them from the Blackbird Hills region in the summer of 1845, where they had to survive on roots and an occasional raccoon or muskrat. Smallpox nearly decimated the entire tribe in 1851. Their population fell from 1,400 (in the late 1830s) to 800 in 1855 (87).*]

In the evenings, we had lamps or they turned the lamps off and we had a wood stove. The center of that wood stove, back by the windows like that, were where you could see the light.

And they'd tell stories. My grandmother told of the coming of Jesus Christ. She called him Wakóⁿda Izhíⁿge. That's God's son. That's how we refer to him. Jesus came later on. That he told them he was real. He showed his hands. His ribs. And he said, "Wakóⁿda izhíⁿge akʰa shábe," which means he was a dark-skinned person. I've always known. That's what I believe. She told of his resurrection, when he was crucified. She told all this in Umóⁿhoⁿ. She had flash cards.[5] We went step by step and she told us of when he came back to life and when he was walking away with his people and where he moved that rock. She had all that, step by step, all in Umóⁿhoⁿ, and when I talked to my kids about this, who told her? Could it have been my grandfather that translated for her? The stories? She was very traditional—had a sweat lodge. My grandfather was a member of the Native American Church. He was very religious. Every Sunday we went to church [*Latter Day Saints in Macy*]—every Sunday. There was acceptance of one creator. That's the way I was brought up. But she also told us stories about Little Red Riding Hood in Umóⁿhoⁿ. There again, my grandfather could have told her those stories. Goldilocks and the Three Bears. What was the other one? Three Little Pigs. But they were all done in Umóⁿhoⁿ, so we knew it. When I went to school and when they read those stories to us, I knew them. She also told us other stories but I was too young to remember them because I'd fall asleep.

[*Alice said she wanted to get back to their general customs and beliefs. One of these beliefs had to do with respect shown toward one's father-in-law, or in a more specific case, toward Alice's male cousin named Harvey. She explained that one day he walked in the door when her grandmother was braiding her hair or "doing something." The grandmother said, "Don't look at him." She*] *obeyed her, not looking or speaking to him to show appropriate respect. That conversation led to the idea of harmony, maintaining and keeping harmony in our lives and homes. Alice called herself "head-of-household." Her husband, Frank, died four years ago, in 2001. She talked of keeping things together, making them work. She said that she and Eleanor (Eleanor's brother, Frank, was Alice's husband so they are related) talk about how they are going to handle things with their respective families. Sometimes this means taking back harsh words before an incident gets out of hand and talking about how to deal with miscommunication that leads to hurt feelings.]*

Brothers and sisters did not talk to each other or look each other in the eyes. They practice it today. One would say, "Gwen, can you tell my sister I want this. Can she do this for me?" And she's going to bring it back to you. And you deliver it to me and say, "Yeah, she can do it. What is it? Give it to me and I'll do something." That was prevention. Those are prevention makers of abuse or any kind. So that's how we did things. Grandmothers and aunties scolded the children. Uncles and grandfathers did the same thing. Grandfathers taught them the knowledge, uncles taught them how to hunt. They taught them this and that. They had the right to scold them. And the parents were the good guys, the ones that comforted them. There's a breakdown there, a big major breakdown in this now. Now we have one-parent households, so that's not there. Who are we? We're the bad guys now. Okay. It's probably that way in your culture, too. Parents are younger. Grandparents are younger. Whatever you have that was handed down to you. What do we do now? Watch TV, watch cartoons. Play games. We didn't do that. That's where the breakdown is and it's not just our people.

Everyone. They're experiencing that. And how are we going to bring some of that back? So our communities can get well. It's not there anymore. We went through a drastic change by the United States government—what they did to us. They oppressed us and we're still experiencing that. So what do we call that? Victimization. They came and they built schools and sent us, took our kids—more or less kidnapped the children and put them in schools. The change came way back with mission schools. The people that came here to this country—lots of change! Diseases that we weren't immune to. Smallpox. Measles. Tuberculosis. That's what my mother died of. Consumption. Twenty-six years old when she passed and I didn't know her. So, here we are today. I have more understanding of how we are. I feel no hate. We got to learn to survive, you know. In our coming days of our ancestors, I'm talking about my mother, grandmother—their role was to make gardens, make food, maintain the children. And today, in this century, we're still doing it. We still are! You are too. We go out and work. We bring the money home. We still go home and manage our homes. We still have to take care of our children. It's still there but we're doing it in a different manner. And I had this traditional man who was really against my working. He thought I should be home taking care of my children. He told me, he said, "Money is false god." Some of them still believe that. I changed that. Money is necessity. We need the money to survive. Look at you. You need money to buy your cigarettes. He smoked. You need money for that little boy, you need the money for that car that has to have gas. I just went on and on about the money—how money is a necessity. I said, "I'm never going to be a millionaire, but I need that money to survive, to support my children, put clothes on them." And now, it's too expensive. Where are they going to get them buckskins? They cost three thousand dollars! So the money is important. I said, "I'm still doing the same thing my grandmother did, making a home, bringing home the bacon." I'm still taking care of my kids and I still respect my husband. But we're more modern now. But we still need to retain some of our ways. Language is one. We need to have our language. It's got to be there. To know who we are. I can say, "Umó^{n}ho^n wa?u bthí^n" [*I'm an Omaha woman*]. It's how to say, I'm a grandmother, great-grandmother.

[*Alice raised what she called three sets of children: the first set are in their forties, the second set are in their late twenties and thirties, and the third set are teenagers in the range of fifteen or so. She said they are all welcome now to come home whenever they want. "Just come home and say 'Hello, how are you?' We have strong family ties," she said. Alice has one great-grandchild, who is two years old, and a granddaughter who is going to be three months old. Her youngest son married a Navajo girl whose grandparents and great-grandparents still live in Arizona. "Even though we're a different tribe, we have similar beliefs," she said. Our conversation drifted back to the importance of language.*]

The language is going to survive. We have people in our community right now who are interested in our language. They want to learn. And it's easier for us, for me, because we teach the Omaha language scientifically. We have our lesson plans and that's how we do it. We take them step by step because they're oriented that way because of the schools. And there's a computer. It's easier to teach them. Small children are going to learn, too. We're getting these CD's and have those available in our classrooms. They listen to them. The first set we had were tapes. For these other students, we have them on CD. Ardis, that's the girl I work with [*at NICC*], she knows all the technology. I feel very lucky and blessed to have somebody like her, and then in turn, we teach each other. The kids are hungry for it. And somewhere along in there, we're going to have speech.

[*Alice felt that the language, as a connector to culture, was the missing link. She qualified this with the statement that to some people, harmony is playing games at home with their children, connecting with them that way.* "We have games we play—cards—and the words are in Umóⁿhoⁿ, and when they win, they say bashéthoⁿ. We have games that we translate in Omaha." *Alice's daughter, Rene, is a certified teacher in Umóⁿhoⁿ. She smiled and told me she was from the "first set."*]

[*There was the question of walking between worlds, of borders and edges that rubbed together, separately, then together again. This was evident in Alice's years in Lincoln, where she lived with her husband and children, working at a number of jobs.*]

I moved to Lincoln in 1965, '66—lived there for twenty-five years. I worked for the Lincoln Action Program for about three years. I was an outreach worker, a community organizer. They had different names at that time. I worked for emergency room medical services. I was an outreach worker for that. I served on many boards there. I was also an emergency food and medical services coordinator. I was on the board of the Lincoln Action Program, the board of the Indian Center. I was involved in everything. The only one I didn't get involved with was the Health Board and Parole Board. I was nominated, voted in, even when I wasn't there! So I was really involved. And when I came back to Macy, I worked as a Child and Family Services worker. I worked with youth.

And I worked as a Youth Court Counselor. [*A youth court counselor lets parents and youth know their rights, gets them an attorney if needed, and fills out affidavits.*]

[*In the seventies, Alice worked for the Housing Tenant Association. They had an office on 27th and Vine and helped people find housing, particularly students attending the University of Nebraska.*]

My first job in Lincoln was babysitting. I applied for jobs. One was a laundry on O Street. There were all Indian women working there. So I went there and they didn't hire me. They said I had poor body movement! Then one day, a truant officer showed up in the morning. One of my brothers-in-law, he's young, he didn't go to school. This lady knocks on the door and walks right in. "C'mon Gary, let's go to school now, get your cap." She just barged in the door and I was sitting at the table. I didn't say anything. And she said, "What are you doing here? Who are you?" I told her who I was. She came back later and hired me for a babysitter for some reverend on 24th Street. She had one baby that was in braces for some reason. I would help her get her ready, get things ready. I think I was making twenty-five, thirty dollars a week.

[*Alice talked about living and working in Lincoln while raising her "first set" of three children. The "second set" came when her husband was a student at the university. "Everyone rotated," she said. The boys were at East High, so they came home, "got things ready and my husband came home from school and he did things and my daughter came back. She was there with the kids and then I came home and took over. I didn't have a babysitter—outside babysitter." Everyone helped. Then her husband became ill.*]

They diagnosed him with diabetes and he had heart problems. He had a heart attack once, but we don't know where, when, how. Nothing. He said, "We're going to go back to Macy—to survive." We've been home some twenty-three years now, maybe twenty-four, something like that. They told him he wasn't going to live to be forty-five. So I made all the decisions, handled everything from that time on, and I still do and I'm glad I did because I'm surviving without him. He's been gone four years now. So he lived twenty years after they said he would. He had a heart attack. His heart was badly damaged. When he left us he was a shell of a man. It's going to be four years this month, February 28. And my children, they did a good job of taking care of him. He was sick twenty-four hours. My youngest daughter was in the Career Ladder program and she pulled out to take care of him, help take care of him. My youngest daughter and my youngest son, they did a good job. Everybody worked together.

I have good memories of growing up out in the rural area [*in Macy*]. I will always treasure those memories of my grandparents. And that school, McCauley, still stands. I see that the bell was still there, but oh, about three, four months ago, we went by there and the bell was gone. It either fell off or someone took it. And the farmers that we went to school with are all scattered out. I don't know where they're living. Some are in Colorado, some in California, Winnebago . . . the farmers back in those days were losing their land like crazy. Some had to move into the cities to survive. The one that was right across from us moved to Omaha. I know some people in Decatur said the lady that we knew passed away last year. And the young lady that I talked about that graduated from that school—she always said "I'm going to come back," which is what she did. She became a teacher. She's somewhere in Decatur or Tekamah, and there's always someone asks about her. One of these days—she might be alive or maybe she isn't. Maybe I walk past her and don't know it. But she was my teacher and all of us that were there, we never called her Miss Ferguson, we called her Punkie because that was her name. So one of these days, maybe I'll run into Punkie. I learned to speak English when I went off to boarding school.

I was about twelve, somewhere in there. My grandfather said to me one day, "You're going to go off to school far away." He said, "You're going to go there to learn from the white people." The reasoning, he said, was that I was going to be a young lady. "I want you to go there and learn because I'm uncomfortable how to tell you. And you're a young lady. You're going to be thirteen." I went there but he never said there's going to be bad. I never experienced a lot of things that these people did. But it's still a shock I guess. I spoke English there. I learned to speak better. I never looked for anything bad about the people that were there. The only negative thing I remember is . . . I had long hair. There's a bunch of us on buses. It's like an airport where you go and say goodbye. And we were there, saying goodbye, saying goodbye, and I see them doing something, but I wasn't sure. When we got close, got close . . . well, I realized what was going on. Yeah, they cut my hair. And they took this white stuff, like flea powder. They sprayed it all over us, everywhere. On my hair, on my clothes. Everything. Then we could go in the building. And I looked at them and I said, "I don't have bugs." Oh, but we have to do this, they said. So to this day, I don't know what they did with my hair because it was long, very beautiful long, long hair. That's the only—I remember that staying with me. I can honestly say that. But you know, we were kids, doing that went away. But it's always still here. Still there. That's my memory of boarding school.

[*She talked about their classes—English, social studies, and history. They had dances—white dances such as ballroom dancing and the Mexican hat dance. She said she also square-danced, and that one time, there was actually a powwow there, but she couldn't go because she wasn't a participant. The ones who did wore their "regalia." In those days, kids didn't go to powwow. We talked about coming back to one's "center," or home place—in Alice's case, back to Macy after over twenty years in Lincoln. Things had changed on the reservation, she noted. Many people living there had red hair or blue eyes but spoke with an Indian accent. "They talk to you and you can tell they're Indian," she said. "I have relatives, cousins now, they're Umóⁿhoⁿ-German. The parents are Umóⁿhoⁿ-German and the kids. She married a white man. They are all successful. The cousin is a doctor—a pediatrician who works in a hospital out east. He's married to a Swede from the old country. They want to be Umóⁿhoⁿ. They got shawls, outfits. They want to be fancy-dancers. But you look at them and you can't tell." She said they are proud to be Umóⁿhoⁿ and she probably wouldn't live to see it, but that there will be a lot of them on the reservation. "We call them half-breeds, even if they're a different tribe, they're still considered half-breeds. But they're proud of their heritage. They want to connect with the Omahas. That is going to be their strength."*

[*On May 16, 2005, I returned to Macy to visit with Alice again in the tribal council building. After meeting briefly, she offered to take me south of Macy, where she grew up, and by her old country school, McCauley. My husband had accompanied me that day and offered to drive us around that portion of the reservation. I felt encumbered at times with my tape recorder. Taping sessions became very informal, but there was always the "idea" of the recorder as an object between us, the tape moving silently, the equipment altering the feeling of the interview to some degree. Even though the women I visited with became used to it and chatted more informally as the session progressed, the objectification of the recorder-tape-microphone could not be ignored.* In The Social Life of Stories, *Julie Cruikshank states that stories became a shared process between those telling and those listening, creating networks of shared experience that move beyond the immediacy of a primary oral narrative. In sharing stories, through interviews with women elders in Macy, my inherited culture (the non-Indian culture) became less rigid and controlling. Cruikshank speaks of this lack of rigidity and control as leading toward stories as "social activities rather than some reified product. We come to view it as part of the equipment for living rather than a set of meanings embedded within texts and waiting to be discovered" (41). She emphasizes that what goes into storytelling is not simply interpretation, because interpretation depends on conceiving of stories as static and written. "The content of oral sources depends on what goes into the questions, the dialogue, the personal relationship through which it is communicated" (40). This was particularly true when I listened to stories of Eleanor, Alice, and Háwate. At first, the dialogue depended on the questions I asked. The questions served as prompts to elicit responses and an ongoing dialogue that was less constrained. But as I became socially involved with these women (a shared and open dialogue rather than a conscripted direction), the stories of their lives opened into other stories, layers upon layers of stories of where they were born, the life situations they encountered, marriages and divorces, children, the loss of children and husbands, jobs, work outside the reservation, and subsequent work inside the reservation.*

[*Key in these stories was the element of what Cruikshank termed "narrators and listeners." One reflects the other, and in this reflection it becomes social and shared—not isolated. Cruikshank also noted the risks and challenges inherent in transcribing from interviews. Even though "voice" and individuation were not lost in transcription, the shared social life of stories was altered. In conversation between individuals, the dialogue is open, ongoing, and spontaneous. It exists in pauses, reflections, and questions. It is spontaneous and can be life-changing when information is moral in content. Once this social process is recorded and transcribed into written form, the performance of stories is lost and then open to interpretation. (*Life Lived Like a Story, *36).*

[*On this occasion, I didn't want to be tied to the presence of the machine. I wanted to listen to Alice in a different way that would not suggest an eventual transcription and hence any altering of shared story.*

[*We drove west, away from Macy, through the fields and past the old school, where I took a picture. As we headed back toward town, away from the country of Alice's childhood, she talked about her husband, Frank. She felt that it was important to have the story of her romance with Frank on tape for her children. I handed her the microphone.*]

He came to my house when I was a teenager. We lived out west, west of Macy here. My cousin, Isabelle Drum, she's deceased now. She brought him over and said, "There's a girl you should meet. She likes to sing, you play the guitar. You meet her." So I went out and talked to him. We met and he started playing the guitar. He asked me to sing. I don't even remember what I sang! And then they left and I didn't see him for a while. Maybe in the fall, maybe Macy powwow. I talked to him—we talked to each other. He said he lived in Lincoln, that his parents moved to Lincoln for jobs. I knew his mother. And I said, "We're still working." We picked corn and the corn we picked was ours. It belonged to us. It was our money. So that's how I was making my money. I was always "the girl with the money," but I was working hard for that money! And then early one morning, a blizzard was happening. The wind was blowing, snow where you couldn't hardly see. I was in the kitchen washing up to eat. My cousin said, "Sasu is coming." I said, "don't lie." She said, "Yeah, put that dish on the table. He's crossing the ditch." I was still in the kitchen, messing around there. "Hurry up and put that plate on. He's at the porch. He's on the porch now." He knocks on the door and we open it. Guess who it was? It was him! He came there to see me in a blizzard. And then, like I said, we put a dish on the table and ate. That's when my grandfather must have realized that we were getting serious. Sometime later, everybody showed up at my father and step-mother's house. They're over there discussing us—my grandpa, my father and my step-mom and his mom and dad, grandmother, who was living at that time. I found out why that meeting was. We were related! That was the relationship they were there to discuss—why we couldn't be married.

[*Alice said her great-grandmother was a Saunsoci and that she didn't know that—Mae Saunsoci. "My grandmother, Alice Miller, that was her mother." The marriage was approved, however, and they got married and moved to Lincoln. "If I had my way," she said, "I don't think I would have been legally married." Both my husband and I laughed, surprised when she said that and asked her why. "I'm going to defend myself, why I said that.*

I think there's some advantages to that because when my husband was seriously ill, we needed this medical help. He wasn't eligible because of me. I was healthy, working. We made too much money. For them, I made too much money." She talked again about the importance of teaching the Omaha language to anyone who wanted to learn, how she wanted this so badly that she went back to school at NICC and graduated in 1991. Alice began teaching Umóⁿhoⁿ in 2000 and continues to be an enthusiastic teacher for language preservation through her students, who speak it to one another and in the community at large.

[*The drive ended at Alice's house, east of Macy. It was a rectangular brick home with the poles of a sweat lodge in the yard. She showed us where she wanted a garden, but that it was too overgrown with weeds. The farmer, she explained, who could plow it for her and turn the soil had not showed up to help. I asked if I could take her picture. She walked over and stood under a tree next to her house. I snapped several pictures and thanked her. As we drove from her house back toward Macy, I realized the difference Alice was making each day as one who was "language-bearer" for her community. She is mother to many, language teacher, and a preserver of words that without her dedication would be lost.*]

5. Háwate, Wenona Caramony

Preserver of Community and Language Advocate

I was born in Macy and lived here all my life, I guess, except for a few years that I was away. The elders, as I was growing up, called me by my Indian name, which is Háwate. So to this day, some of the elders still call me that. And now I notice some of the young ones call me that. I belong to the Buffalo Clan— $I^nk^hésabe\ wa?ú\ bthi^n$.[1] My grandfather was Amos Mitchell, and my grandfather on my mother's side was named Andrew Liep. My grandmother was Mabel Fremont Mitchell, and I am not sure of my grandmother on my dad's side.

My grandfather on my father's side—see, his father has the right to give the Indian name to children—that is how I got my name. Háwate interprets to mean the traditional dress of the Omaha woman.[2] It's a two-piece dress. The skirt has pleats around it, and the women wore slips with real pretty lace on it. And then there was a broach that you wore with

Háwate, Wenona Caramony

your dress, and my mother used to say, when a woman is really dressed up, she'll wear a choker of black beads. (I don't have any on.)

And usually they're long and they a have a gathered pleat around the edge. I remember seeing all the Omaha women wear those kind of dresses as I was growing up. They don't wear them as much now—only on special occasions. Well, some of the women wear them at social dances and at pow-wows, and some of the women that are in the Native American Church wear them also.

I learned to speak the Omaha language through my grandpa because I used to sleep in the same room with him. That was my Omaha grandpa, yeah, I loved him. I used to go over to my aunt's quite a bit and visit her, walk over there. And a lot of times, I'd stay with her. That's how come I had my bed in his room. And my aunt didn't have children. She used to walk me to school. I remember every one of us had chores to do. She had a schedule. Somebody had to wash dishes, somebody had to cook, get kindling for the fire next morning. Just everything. We gardened. She used to buy maybe two hundred baby chicks and she'd raise them until they got to be fryers. Then sold them off. I helped with that. Most of the time, though, I'd wash dishes. I had a sister that liked to cook, so she got to cook all the time. But we took turns at different jobs. We helped with gardening in the beginning, but after it got weedy, nobody wanted to go out there. I remember we used to send Rudy out there to dig potatoes. [*She laughed at the memory.*] We grew string beans, corn . . . I think she canned it. But we ate it right along, you know? My Aunt Lizzie, my mother's sister, she used to can. They'd kill a hog. And then she'd can all that meat. I remember she'd can them in jars for the winter. She used a pressure cooker. There used to be broth in it.

I used to take care of my grandpa because he was blind and only had one arm, so I remember I used to roll his cigarettes. At night, he used to tell me stories and he'd say, "I'm going to tell you stories, but every now and then, I want you to say 'huuh' so whenever you stop saying that I'll know you're asleep." That was his way of putting me to sleep, I guess. These stories he told were called *hígas*. He only told them in the winter when there was snow on the ground. And I'm sorry to say I don't hardly remember any of them. But I knew they were good stories. And each story had a moral to it.

I'm the eldest of eight children. There were three boys and five girls, and we grew up very poor and very sheltered by a mother who didn't take us anywhere except on certain occasions. But we spent most of our time out in the country [*around Macy*] where we had our own fun playing cards and a croquet set. I remember we had those. That was entertainment. And then if she did take us anywhere, we had to sit still. We couldn't run around. So, anytime she took us we all sat still because we were so happy to get to go somewhere. Growing up, until I was a teenager, I remember just living in army tents. I don't remember living in a house until I became a teenager. Then I think the government built us a two-room house, and that was the first house I remember. Other than that, we always lived in an army tent. No kind of facility. But we were happy, I guess.

I live about three miles north of here, out in the country. But I remember living in several places because my grandpa had land here and there. We just kind of moved, like gypsies. I had a mother that believed in education. I remember how she'd always tell us that you must get your education, go to school. That's the only way you're going to make it out into the white man's world. And she'd always talk Indian.

There was both Umóⁿhoⁿ and English spoken in our home, but I think mostly Indian. See, my mother was what you call a half-breed, but she spoke fluent Omaha language. She was a good fluent speaker. I attended the school here at Macy, but it burned down. Then I went to the Indian school at Flandreau, South Dakota—boarding school. I graduated from there. Like I say, being sheltered and not going anywhere—once I got away and saw other things I really didn't want to come back. So in the summer, that first summer at Flandreau, I went on what they called "outing." I went on an outing to Sioux Falls, South Dakota, and worked for a lady that had a business selling hats. I took care of her dad, too. And then that fall, I came home for awhile. Then I got accepted at Haskell Institute, where they took commercial training there. So for the next two years I went there—to Haskell. Haskell is in Lawrence, Kansas.[3] From there, I got married. I didn't come home. My boyfriend was in the Navy so we got married. I went with him, followed him around, stayed with him, and out of this marriage I had four children. They were all born in the military. We did a lot of traveling. We lived mostly on the East Coast. A few times we went to the West Coast, but it was Florida to Rhode Island, along the coast. [*She laughed.*] I always tell my children they're military brats.

[*I asked her if she got homesick and thought of Eleanor and Alice, moving away from Macy, Eleanor at seven years of age and Alice as a young woman. I thought of all the years they spent away from their place of birth and childhood and of their return.*]

I didn't really get homesick. I guess I had my children to keep me busy. Then too, I liked the military life . . . meeting all these Navy wives, and we all kind of had our own little thing going. I enjoyed the military life. My oldest child is Loretta. She is about a senior citizen, and there's Rosa. She's about ready to be a senior citizen, too. And then there's Donald. And Norman. They're around here in Macy, all doing very well. Except my oldest daughter is not too well. And my second daughter is handicapped, but she did very well for herself. She went to college and owns her own home there in Omaha.

I grew up with my mother and siblings. My father left us when we were, I don't know what year, but we were all young.

I was much older than the others. But I remember our father left us because of alcoholism and my mother just raised us by herself. I always think how she gave up so much of her life to raise us kids because she worked. She'd even walk about three miles to catch a bus up to the four-corners area. She caught the bus to Macy from where we lived.

My brothers were Clement, Kenneth, and Rudi. My sisters were Happy, Glenna, Octa, and Vivian. Two of my brothers are deceased. I have a sister that is deceased, too. She lived in Seattle, Washington. And I have a sister that lives in St. Louis and two sisters living in Omaha. My brother lives in Omaha. By the way, I should call him Doctor Mitchell I guess. [*Rudi Mitchell has a doctorate in education and a masters degree in social work.*] I still see my siblings. I'm fortunate that way. I don't see them often but I do get to see them every now and then and I know they're not too far away now. My sister, the one that died who lived in Seattle, we seldom got to see her. I guess what I'm trying to tell you is, when I left here, I just left. I must have been away from the reservation for about twenty-six years. Like I told you, I got married and I lived in Hawaii with my children, traveled on a big luxury ship which was really nice. Everything on that ship. I remember my first scene of Hawaii. My husband asked me to look through that porthole. And I looked and could see those hula girls dancing as we were ready to get off. I always remember that. We lived over there. We were just accepted because I looked Hawaiian—Hawaiian-Chinese. But my two girls took lessons there. They became hula dancers—really good hula dancers. The teacher used to say it was a natural for them because she thought they were Hawaiian. I was over there three years. And I was there when it became a state, so I remember all the bonfires around the beach. I loved it there! I'd go back if I had the chance. After my husband retired, after putting twenty-three years in, I came back to the reservation. Shortly after, because of alcoholism, we went our separate ways. Divorced.

[*Háwate married a Sioux man named Robert Moran.*]

I had a daughter, which I always say was a gift from God to me, because she has stayed with me and she's young and really watches over me now. Lani. I gave her a Hawaiian name. Lani means "a child from heaven." She is thirty-five now and doing very well for herself. She has a good job and owns her own home in Horton, Kansas. I make a trip down there now and then to see her. She works at a big casino there so I go down and have a good time. When I came back, I went to NICC. I was one of the first graduates there, I think. I got my degree there and then I took an eighteen-month course in being a paralegal. That training took me to law school in Louisville, Kentucky. Then I studied Indian law at the University of New Mexico. The tribal council hired me as a judge for I think three years. My responsibility was what you call a juvenile judge. And then I also did the primary sentencing and all that. There were a few of us that took this training, and when we came back, we changed the whole court system. Prior to that, there was just one judge doing everything. Each one [*juvenile*] had a public defender and a prosecutor and judge. I took the training and then we came back and changed everything. Before that, it was what was called a kangaroo court, I guess. But today, the court is run with rights for people. I remember working for the Community Action Program. It was a program for low-income people. I got involved in that. They trained me to be a community

organizer. From that, I had training where they sent me to
Peru State for one summer. Then one summer I went to Kansas University. One year I went to Briar Cliff in Sioux City.
I got a lot of training through them, too. I worked with the
tribal council and later became education director, taking
care of all the programs like boarding schools, college—also
the Johnson O'Malley director, I did education programs for
Indian students.

The boarding schools were called BIA schools, Bureau of
Indian Affairs, and Flandreau in South Dakota was one of
them.[4] There was also Wahpeton, North Dakota, and then
Pierre Learning Center. That was one of the BIA schools. But
I served on all the school boards on those and took care of
the children that went there. I used to make monthly visits to see them. It was a nice experience for me because I
cared. I wanted them to be happy at why they were there. I
wanted them to stay in school, so my concern was there. I like
that work very much. I also became a member of the school
board here in Macy, so I got elected. I have an adopted son—
Dennis Hastings. He's the historian for the tribe. He and I
decided we'd run for the Macy school board. And we made
it. Because the reason we were running is we wanted our language to be a part of the curriculum here at the school. We got
that done and he resigned, but I stayed on. I've been on the
school board several times off and on. At one time, I resigned
my position to run Title V. It's now Title VI, I think. But at
the time, it was Title V. That was teaching our language and
culture to our students here at Macy. I also taught language
at the community college here at Macy and then at the South
Sioux campus. At present, I teach the Omaha language at the
Walthill Public School. My commitment is to leave as much

of the language behind me. I'm getting older. I got to thinking about my classmates that I used to have. How many are
still living? And I can't think of any that are.

[*I asked her how she saw her role in the community. She said
she liked to be known as "Grandma," as a language teacher.*]

I had an uncle that passed away here, oh, about a year now.
Uncle Ty. But two years before he passed away, I was visit-
ing with him. We were talking Indian, you know, and he
said, "Háwate, we're getting old now." He wanted me to be
strong. Keep on going. I always remember those words now
that he's gone. He was always kind of—if I needed anybody
to talk to, he was always my counselor. I miss him very much.
But then I think how he told me to be strong and keep going. That I will do.

[*A typical work day for Háwate consists of bringing her grandson to school, then going to work at Walthill as the language
teacher. For relaxation, she goes to social dances and eats with
"my seniors" at the senior center in Macy. "I like to go to the casino, too," she added. The social dances were held at the community center west of the tribal council building. "We like to
have visitors come," she said. Vida talked about Háwate's role
in the Minute Women Organization and asked if she would ex-
plain it to me.*]

The Minute Women was organized in 1944 for the sake of
our military boys and girls. Whenever they come home, they
welcome them, have a big social dance and just be happy that
they're back. This was organized by three women. They're
my aunts. We're all related. Their names are Florence Merrick, Minnie Woodhall Parker, and Mary Lieb Mitchell. I remember my mother saying that they went on horse and buggy
down south [*south of the reservation*] to see Charlie Parker, an

elder, who is kind of a medicine man, to get his permission to start this organization. That's how the organization started. Mama, my mother, used to say, "Well, I named the organization Minute Women because I thought of the Revolutionary War—the Minute Men, you know. So I called it the Minute Women." They did things on the spur of the moment. If a military boy or girl came home, they didn't say [*they would celebrate*] at such and such a date. They did it right now. Food and drink. They had a good time with them.

[*Vida, also a member of the organization, told me that often they would have a hand game*[5] *or dinner to honor the service person. Háwate said the organization is still going, that the "offsprings" do it now. We left the subject of the Minute Women to talk about Háwate's mother, who was not only a role model for her but the inspiration for her life.*]

She was a very active woman, a go-getter, a disciplinarian. Strict. Protective. She always stressed education. I guess that's why my family is educated. She used to say, "you're going to have to cope with whites, you know, live in the white man's world. You have to be educated," she'd say.

I have a little business of my own now, too, in my home. I started this about ten years ago. It's not anything you get rich on. But I thought it would be nice to have something on the reservation. We're always looking for blankets—all kinds of blankets for giveaways and for funerals. So I decided I would have one of those kind of businesses where I provide the blankets and they can just come and pick whatever they want. I send for them from two places—Texas and Kentucky. My job is to pay the bills! If they want blankets for giveaways, I have them and they just pay me for them. I've been doing this about ten years now. And I used to be the Avon lady for about fifteen years. I love doing Avon. And I go to meetings as part of the Macy school board called NAFIS, National Association of Federally Impacted Schools.[6] There's all kinds of jobs connected with trying to get money for the school, like bond issues. I like teaching the language the most of all these jobs. We have a curriculum. Maybe for a few weeks, it's the numbers and colors. A lot of it is repetitious and it's not writing. It's just how I say it. That's the way I teach. Because if it's in writing, the kids, they look all over before they have to say a word or something. They look all over and I say, "No, don't look," I just take everything down.

[*She turned to Vida and expressed her enthusiasm for her grandson, Josh, and* the way he was using the language.] "He is doing real good! The other day I asked him, "Mí idón^{b}e áno^n?" He asked me first and I said, "Thí!, míido^{n}be áno^n a?" [You! What time is it?] He went and looked and he said it right. "Wí thé sáto^n, wí thé tákita." Four-thirty. So he's catching on real good. I've been talking more and more to him, too. "Mí thé dón^{b}e sáto^n, mí théde tákita"—it means past. You could say it that way, too. But if it's right on the dot at four-thirty, you'd say "widét^{h}o^n."

I remember every summer my dad used to Indian dance. My mom did too. Every summer, we used to go up to the Dales at Wisconsin. There was a campground there for tourists. My father and mother, they danced. And I had a sister, Vivian, who dressed in buckskin. She was little, but she had a nice voice on her. And she'd sing. But I remember going to those every summer. I remember looking forward to those. The whole family went. We stayed all summer. Then on the way back, we'd stop and pick cranberries. That was cranberry season. I think they picked it and sold it to the farmer. He paid them.

I don't know how much he paid them, but I remember that. As the oldest of the children, I stayed home with the kids every now and then. My mother always worked—for the teachers here—and did housework. But I remember I used to stay home with the kids. We'd all take care of each other.

[*Vida mentioned that one of Háwate's responsibilities of being a Buffalo Clan woman was marking the cake, a special kind of cake—wedding, birthday, graduation, memorial cakes. She explained that families pick certain buffalo women that belong to the clan to cut the cake. It was an honor, but also what she called "a big job." Vida (also an Iⁿkʰésabe) said they make sure the food gets out to the people. "And all this is symbolic of buffalo. We used to hunt them all the time. Making sure everybody had their portion."*]

And when I cut the cake, I like to make sure that everybody gets a piece. I have a certain way of passing that cake around. I start form the east door and go clockwise. I go to the drummers first, then the center. From there it goes to the east door and on around clockwise. I try to cut the cake so everybody gets a piece. It can be difficult because there can be so many cakes! I remember one time, I cut seven cakes at one gathering. They were big ones, too. Bigger than normal. I always tell my grandson, they honored me with cutting a cake. They don't take into consideration that I'm old! [*Vida told me that prior to cutting them, Háwate had to take them around so if there were seven cakes, they all had to be shown to the people.*]

I'm going to be eighty-one years old this year. To me, it's like history is repeating itself for me, like being on the school board. I'll be on there for the next four years if I last that long. I think I've been on the board for about twenty-some years.

[*"She works here with the language program. She's been involved with the school a long time as an educator," Vida commented.*]

I forgot about my late husband. He's been gone for about six years now. When I met him, I was the tribal judge. And he didn't want me to be the judge, so that's how come I resigned and got married. He was a real traditional man. Nice man. But he believed in traditional ways. So he asked my mother if he could take me. Went over to the house. Rudy was sitting there in the room. Mama said Rudy wanted to leave but she made him stay. He asked my mother if he could take me in marriage. He was good for me, good for her, too. Because when he bought me my first overshoes, she said, "Oh, I know he's taking care of my girl." All my grandchildren—that was the only grandpa they knew. They just loved him. When he passed away, they all just took it so hard. But I was always thankful he was around. He used to talk to them like they were his own grandchildren. He was one of those men that was what we call "staff carriers" for the Native American Church. The staff carriers are like priests—you can go to them anytime and ask for advice. My father went to the Native American Church. Children don't go. Only adults. [*"Sometimes people will take their children," Vida said. I reminded Háwate of another story she might want to tell. There was one about a "medicine lady" named Betsy Hastings who was an elder. "Betsy told a story about her grandmother who didn't speak English very well. Once she went to the phone and said, 'Operation, give me long ways.'" Háwate laughed. "There are a lot of stories like that," she said, "but I remember that one because I thought it was real cute." I was still curious about the "goose story."*]

A long time ago, the store owner let you charge food if you didn't have any money. Credit. He got concerned once when this lady was going to be able to pay him. She told him, "My grandma here says she's going to pay you when the geese come back." And the owner said, "I don't give a heck when the geese come back. How about right now?" Macy used to have a store that burned down. It's gone. I remember the post office used to be right on the corner, across from the old post office. Used to be kind of a high bank where it sat. I remember a gas station right on the corner. That's all gone. The store used to be called the GI Store. There were two veterans that came here and started it. So they called it the GI Store.

Another story I heard is about the fox and the geese. The fox saw all these geese down below and he was hungry. So he came down to where the geese were. He talked to them. He had a small drum with him, too, so he told them he was going to sing them songs and he wanted them to dance around him. But they had shut their eyes as they were dancing around him. He would sing them songs and as they came closer to him, he would grab one by the neck, strangle it, and put it in his sack. So he was catching them right and left. And there was one geese that opened her eyes and she saw what he was doing, and she hollered and said, "Run! He's going to kill all of us!" The remaining geese all got away. The moral of the story is that you should always have your eyes open, see what's going on. Each story had a moral to it.

I think I'm very fortunate to cope with two worlds. Diversity. I remember when I worked for the tribe, I'd go to a meeting. I like to dress up so I'd dress up and then I'd come back home here to Macy and get back to my traditional way of living. I'm always thankful that I'm able to do that. Vida, too. She has to cope with that. Sometimes we'd be the only Indians there at a meeting. I'm used to being among white people. It doesn't bother me. But I imagine it would be hard for some people that aren't used to it. [*"Some of the young people go off and go to school, then make their way back," Vida said. "Some try to go to college. They go through culture shock and come back within a half a year or so. Then some probably manage both lives."*]

Umóⁿhoⁿ Nation Public School [*also known as Macy Public School*] has a long history of teaching culture and language. Elders began teaching culture and language in the public school setting beginning in the 1970s. Emphasis then and now continues to be to produce culturally relevant materials. Efforts include booklets in Umóⁿhoⁿ written by students, with translations provided by the elders. Audio and visual recordings took place in the 1970s and continue in the ULCC today. Umóⁿhoⁿ Nation Public School has long understood that it must promote opportunities for our children to learn directly from their grandmothers and grandfathers.

From the early 1970s to present there have been over fifty elders and community people who have taught at Macy Public School (MPS) and Umóⁿhoⁿ Nation Public School (UNPS). The goal of teaching our children by community input has been a longstanding mission of our school for almost forty years. [*I wondered where things would head in the future.*]

I think they're going to try to educate themselves. They're becoming more aware of getting an education. But we have to instill in them that it is the way to go. I know I try to encourage a lot of our young people to go out. I guess I'm an advocate. Education. I say that because one man introduced me as that—an advocate. We've got to preserve the language.

If the parents don't do it, then we're kind of at a loss I think. There's a big gap between speakers and nonspeakers. Then you have a whole era of active listeners that understand but don't speak. That's what our department tries to find is active listeners—to bring them to speech, give them opportunities to work here. And then work with the children and also they learn methods of language instruction while they're here.

[*Vida said that Háwate teaches the children to say a prayer in Umóⁿhoⁿ.*] And when we go through that, the children are real reverent. They must know that. They probably pray at home, too, or they're taught that. When I pray with them, they hold their hands and some shut their eyes and they just—it's real sincere.

[*I mentally traced Háwate's travels and return to the reservation. I wanted to know, after life beyond the reservation, how she adjusted to her return. Háwate said she had had enough of military life and was happy to get back. All three women's stories had to do with the importance of return to a place of origin—a place not only of roots but of cultural and spiritual relocation. A portion of their individual identity was based on stories of this return to place and a distinct homecoming. In addition, Eleanor, Alice, and Háwate took jobs to ensure cultural survival, which moved them beyond individual identity with roots in Macy to the larger community identity reflected in tribal politics and language preservation. Their life stories represented a circular and dynamic presence that emphasized this identification. Thomas King quotes N. Scott Momaday in* The Truth About Stories *as saying that being Native is an idea that an individual has of themselves and then carries this idea further. "He is acknowledging that language and narrow definitions of culture are not the only ways identity can be constructed" (55).*]

[*Vida and I shut off our equipment. I disconnected the external microphone and put everything away. We stood up and went into the larger space of Vida's office, where chairs were placed around the desks for elder speakers when they stopped by to help teach or visit. Around the corner is the culture center—a round room that invites space and harmony, a place where the Omaha language is spoken and learned. Háwate posed in the center for photographs, draping the blanket her mother made (which contained ribbon designs in bright colors) around her shoulders. The blanket lay in folds against her traditional Omaha Indian dress.*

[*The gift of her narratives seemed woven in the cloth of her dress. It was a land of many dreams, both contextual and textual. In the cloth was the fabric of a multitude of generational stories. In the stories was the power of return to anchor one back to the land, back to language, back to place. It was eternal.*]

Conclusion

It has been many months since I have been to Macy to see Eleanor, Alice, and Háwate. Without this contact, I feel deprived of the friendship of these women I got to know well over the many months of storytelling. This shared space preempted any cultural barriers and allowed for connections that might otherwise not have taken place. Since Eleanor's election to the office of chair of the Omaha tribal council, it has been even harder to negotiate a return to see her and share stories. These stories are not those recorded or transcribed, but stories shared in social dialogue about our lives and our connections to one another through the process of telling life stories. Julie Cruikshank related that storytelling has intrigued students of human behavior for generations from the Arctic to the South Pacific (1990, 154). In her work with three Yukon women elders, she stated that "the recurring theme [of Native women's stories] is one of connection—to other people and to nature" and emphasized the extent to which stories told orally can enlarge understanding of the past (1998, 3). Life stories can also be a springboard from which cultural connections and a return to place lead to reidentification with the self and who that "self" is in the framework of place.

What impressed me in the lives of these three women was how story related to nature (land as sacred and as redemptive in the sense of return) and how it enlarged not only my understanding of their traditional Omaha culture but their understanding of who they were as Omaha women. Throughout, I sensed pride and a desire to do whatever it took to preserve their cultural heritage. Beyond the immediacy of the individual narrative, the communal narrative was quite clear: involvement in tribal politics and language preservation. Just as Cruikshank's recordings of Yukon women elders allowed for further understanding of historicity and place on the part of both teller and listener, my recordings of Omaha women elders allowed me to see deeper into their cultural history. Implicit in this understanding is trust that the narratives will be truthfully rendered, unaltered in the process of transcription (in a monologic or dominant culture sense) and preserved as the stories were told. Textual accuracy was principal.

Also revealed in the life stories was reconnection to the past through a physical return to place. The stories began with birth in a certain location and continued with events of childhood, then described moving to Lincoln or traveling to various locations, as with Háwate's story of marrying a military man and her subsequent life in Hawaii, then culminated with a return to Macy. This physical return to Macy was a decisive event that changed the lives of all three women and was reflected powerfully in their stories in a variety of ways. Alice's husband, Frank, sought a return to Macy to face dwindling health. As a result, Alice focused even more strongly on her goal to graduate from the Nebraska Indian Community College and teach the Omaha language—not only to help her community but also to assist financially in sustaining the family. The story of who she was and who she became through this process meant a reconnection to Macy in a different sense: first through physical return, then through cultural and individual reidentification. Eleanor was content in her home in Lincoln and surprised that her husband wanted to move back to Macy. Her physical return to the home of her birth (even the drive to the house where she was born) framed the self-identification of a woman involved in tribal politics and in making a difference in the lives of the Omaha people. Her stories allowed for this evolution. What was apparent in her narrative was how a return to place was vital in order for this identification to take place. Háwate was initially content to move between the worlds of non-Indian and Indian. As the layers of her story unfolded, her commitment to maintaining language as a means to preserve culture and make young people proud of their Omaha heritage meant a return was necessary—an emotional return focused on remaining in a physical place that was part of her history and culture.

Land and return are paramount in Indigenous stories. Cruikshank noted how "annexations of territories, extraction of minerals, and layers of bureaucratic administration have exerted pressures both on land and on long-standing institutions associated with kinship" (1998, 158). Eleanor talked about "my land," and the elements of her life story emphasized this powerful connection to place. The tragedies of disenfranchisement of Native lands into the hands of non-Indian settlers and colonizers has long been evident in a developed landscape now implicated in extinctions of nature in all its various forms and in land used for profit instead of preservation. When Alice and Eleanor drove me around Macy to show me their childhood beginnings and tell stories about it, I was acutely aware of their connections to land and place.

Land becomes a landscape for Indigenous life stories. In the textual landscape that is composed of language, there is a recognition (based on shared social performances and dialogues between those listening and those telling) that beneath the words is a commitment to restoration based on land, a kind of sacred space. As sacred space, it is reinstated through language and reconnection by telling life stories. Harold Innis referred to this idea when relating the story of a Yukon boy who said he wanted to grow up and become a "land claims negotiator" (Cruikshank, *The Social Life of Stories*, 159). The boy was in a primary school classroom and a visitor had asked what the children hoped to do when they finished school. Land issues and identification with land as sacred space remain dominant in Native life stories. What I learned was that through the process of sharing and telling life stories, reconnections to land became a way of grounding the individual in a space that is forever changing and often threatened.

Inherent in any study where stories are recounted, shared, recorded, and transcribed is the risk taken when hearing again through the transcription process, of attempting to reinterpret the words and thus change the landscape of text and meaning. There is also the risk of placing academic constraints and scholarly implications on what are first and foremost the stories of human lives. How can this terrain be negotiated while respecting the legitimacy of oral narrative? Yet, if stories remain isolated, what is their chance for survival? What will happen to us, as a human community, if risks are not taken to hear, understand, and see each other's life events? The power of story lies in how human lives are not only endured but become shared processes, uniting instead of dividing. To not risk sharing them is to deny who we are and who we will become.

Alice Saunsoci, Eleanor Baxter, and Háwate consistently made the best of things in their lives, lives in transition, much as Leslie Silko's main characters do in *Gardens in the Dunes*. She writes about alienation, assimilation, and return through the eyes of her main characters, Sister Salt and her younger sister Indigo, of the Sand Lizard People. When they are children, Sister Salt and Indigo live with Grandma Fleet in the dune country near Needles, California. In this country, the world is complete and intact. Food is grown, nurtured, stored. They learn to survive on a land that provides melons, amaranth, corn, and beans. "Grandma Fleet explained which floodplain terraces were well drained enough to grow sweet black corn and speckled beans. The squashes and melons were water loves, so they had to be planted in the bowl-shaped area below the big dune where the runoff soaked deep into the sand. Wild gourds, sunflowers, and datura seeded themselves wherever they found moisture" (49). Grandma Fleet attempts to anchor her granddaughters to land and place but cannot hold them there. She dies in the dune country and is buried under an apricot seedling, leaving them to fend for themselves in the outside world of assimilation—a world opposite that of the dune country. Silko wove a story of nature violated as whites show up in hoards to dam the Colorado River, cutting down old and majestic cottonwoods and willows, inundating land with construction workers who violate land and nature in the effort to create a giant aqueduct to funnel water to Los Angeles. Tent cities were built where work for profit became the rule. Humans scourge the landscape like locust hoards, overusing and overextending land in their greed to consume food and water. The restructuring of an entire river for the aqueduct cuts, marks, and decimates nature. There are no gardens here.

Sister Salt and Indigo must work at whatever they can find in the world of dominance that in turn dominates nature. Their survival depends on this assimilation. It is a world of opposites: the dune country where the two found solace and comfort and the broader dominant culture that sought to own, change, and consume. In the end, Silko brought her characters back to the dune country, to the bones of their grandmother, to what had previously sustained them. Upon their return, they discovered that the apricot trees that once sheltered Grandma Fleet's body have been cut down and destroyed, but there is hope in replanting, to nourish and appreciate what is there, to work with land instead of against it. Concurrent with the dune garden is the preservation of the Snake Lizard People. The rattler that lived near the pond created a sacred, rather than poisonous presence—a presence that no longer exists. "Strangers had come to the old gardens at the spring. For no reason, they slaughtered the big old rattlesnake who lived there" (478). Silko ended with the hopeful presence of "Old Snake's beautiful daughter" who is seen drinking at the spring. "She stopped drinking briefly to look at sister, then turned back to the water; then she gracefully turned from the pool across the white sand to a nook of bright shade" (479). The gardens in the dunes eventually thrive. They become, in her writings of recrimination and racial violence against Indians, an optimistic presence in a world dominated by greed. But underlying the story are ever-present themes of alienation, assimilation, and return.

Like Sister Salt and Indigo, Alice, Háwate, and Eleanor lived outside their traditional Native lands but returned to the place that nourished them. The shadowland of mainstreaming and acculturation exist but peripherally alongside the greater presence of Macy at this time in their lives. Like the dune country, Macy can be sustained by nurturing what is already there and allowing for regrowth and restoration: economic restoration, land preservation, and continued emphasis on education. The replanting may mean economic growth, land preservation, continued emphasis on education, and perhaps mainstreaming as Eleanor suggested then returning home to use what has been learned. Like the damming of the Colorado River, the world of cities and towns outside Macy continues to consume land and resources. What will remain? Stories preserve what is there, and like Silko's tale of loss and return, find reverence in survival. Stories endure and become, like the dune country, a place of security.

Toward the end of our interview, Háwate's story of the fox, told by her grandfather, contained trickster motifs common in Native American stories where trickster is representative of both balance and chaos. Trickster in Vizenor's literature "is reflected in origin stories and tales such as 'Naanabozho and the Gambler' and appears as ethos, persona and fictional characters" (Blaeser 1996, 137). Trickster is both comic and tragic culture hero and comprises many forms, obtaining many physical manifestations.

When Háwate told this story, the fox symbolized for me the ignorance that exists between distinct cultural entities where predilections occur for one's own culture. The fox represented an absence of words, a signifier of non-language. Without language, without the "social life of stories" as connectors between disparate worlds where understanding is limited, preconceived notions create distance that cannot be crossed. Like the geese fighting to keep their eyes open, personal life stories, shared in social contexts, create understanding and open dialogue, a discourse that continues long after the recorder is stopped. These stories opened my eyes. They became a way to "see what's going on," to circumvent bifurcations of meaning between Indian and non-Indian cultures. Without this shared presence and performance of orality, narration, and storytelling, it is like singing and dancing with one's eyes closed, hearing only the drums but not understanding the meaning behind them. Long after the dust of Yellow Smoke Road in Macy had been driven from my car tires and I had reentered Lincoln, I still heard the voices of these women. They spoke in silences and non-silences, in words that opened worlds and closed distance.

Notes

Preface

1. Omaha tribal homelands are located in the northeast corner of Nebraska, overlapping a small portion of western Iowa. The area is comprised of the Omaha Tribal Reservation and adjacent counties, totaling 2,594 square miles. The Nebraska counties are Thurston, Burt, Cuming, and Wayne; the Iowa county is Menoma (see Omaha Tribe, "Tribal Indian Child Welfare").

2. Omaha language classes consisted of Omaha I, II, III, and IV and were also taught by linguist Rory Larson and Omaha speakers Alberta Canby and Emmaline Sanchez.

3. Researchers at the University of Nebraska–Lincoln work in conjunction with the university's Institutional Review Board. The board requests that regard and respect be given to any research involving "human subjects." This includes interview subjects. I therefore had to get the permission of the Omaha tribal council to proceed with any project design involving interviews.

4. In June 1981, the North Central Association of Colleges and Schools approved the Nebraska Indian Community College for accreditation at the associate degree level. NICC today serves the Omaha and Santee Sioux tribes of Nebraska at the Macy and Santee campuses.

5. This form was primarily to satisfy Institutional Review Board specifications for research using "human subjects." Chairman Grant, as he was signing the document, said, "I think you need to speak with the IRB about the term they use ["human subjects"]; it is very demeaning to us as a community." I agreed.

6. According to Fletcher and La Flesche (*Omaha Tribe*, 219), Xthéxthe was the name of the "Mark of Honor" tattooed on a girl by her father or near of kin who had won, through certain acts, entrance into Hónhewachígaxe and had secured the right to have this mark tattooed on the girl. Eleanor explained to me that these marks were made when girls were very young, around twelve years old. The tattoos on her mother were located on the arms, the small of her back, and on her forehead. Eleanor told me how painful it had been for her grandmother when these marks were made in the 1860s.

3. Eleanor Baxter

1. According to information in "Omaha Tribal Indian Child Welfare" (2000), the Omaha land base consists of the following: agriculture, 14,784 acres; grazing, 2,446; forestry, 4,042; other, 9,876; total 31,148 acres.

4. Alice Saunsoci

1. The ceremonies of three subgentes of the Thátadas were connected with the growth and care of the maize. The

Wazhí^{n}ga subgens assisted in protecting crops from devastation by birds, and the Kéin ceremonies were connected with rain. The Wasábe subgens shared in ceremonies that pertained to the awakening of spring (Fletcher and La Flesche, *Omaha Tribe*, 159).

2. Decatur is located next to the Missouri River along Highway 75, sixty miles north of Omaha. Lyons is located approximately twenty-three miles southwest of Macy in Burt County.

3. According to Fletcher and La Flesche, *síthede* refers to "heel." *Bazu* means "to point" or "to project." *Síthede bazu* together means "projecting heel."

4. *Teska* means "cow"; *tanúka* means "fresh meat." *Bthat^{h}e* is the first person singular of the verb *that^{h}e*, "to eat," and *go^{n}btha* is the first person singular of the verb *go^{n}tha*, "to want."

5. Mormons, or members of the Church of Latter Day Saints, who were in the area at the time used flash cards to tell stories.

5. Háwate, Wenona Caramony

1. The word *bthé* is the first person singular of the verb *the*, meaning "I am"; *wa?u* means "woman"; and *i^{n}k^{h}ésabe* means "black shoulder," or the back shoulder portion of the buffalo. Háwate says, "I am a Black Shoulder Buffalo Clan woman."

2. *Ha* means "hide"; *wate* means "dress."

3. Haskell Institute was founded in 1882 by the U.S. government as an industrial or trade school for the education of Indian boys and girls.

4. The Bureau of Indian Affairs is staffed predominantly by white people and is charged with the operation of Indian

agencies as well as numerous social service organizations such as welfare agencies, alcohol treatment centers, and law enforcement bureaus.

5. The Omaha hand game is played with two competing sides, normally arranged in a circle with drummers in the middle. There are designated feather carriers and stone carriers. The stone carriers give stones to players who hide them behind their back. The job of the feather carrier is to guess which hand holds the stone. The carrier will indicate this by the position of the feather, pointed at the person holding the stone. The feather carriers go back and forth between the two sides; points are kept with sticks at the head table.

6. NAFIS is a nonprofit, nonpartisan corporation of school districts from throughout the United States organized primarily to educate Congress on the importance of impact aid. Founded in 1973, NAFIS ensures that federally connected children (such as those residing on Indian lands) have adequate federal funds for education.

Works Cited

Anzaldua, Gloria. *Borderlands La Frontera: The New Mestiza*. San Francisco: Aunt Lute Books, 1987.

Bell, Betty Louise. *Faces in the Moon*. Norman: University of Oklahoma Press, 1994.

Blaeser, Kimberly. *Gerald Vizenor: Writing in the Oral Tradition*. Norman: University of Oklahoma Press, 1996.

Cruikshank, Julie. *Life Lived Like a Story: Life Stories of Three Yukon Native Elders*. Lincoln: University of Nebraska Press, 1990.

————. *The Social Life of Stories*. Lincoln: University of Nebraska Press, 1998.

Dorsey, James Owen. *Omaha Sociology*. Washington DC: Government Printing Office, 1884. Reprint, New York and London: Johnson Reprint Corporation, 1970.

Fletcher, Alice, and Francis La Flesche. *The Omaha Tribe*. 2 vols. Annual Report of the Bureau of American Ethnology to the Secretary of the Smithsonian Institution, vol.

27. Washington DC: 1911. Reprint, Lincoln: University of Nebraska Press, 1972, 1992.

King, Thomas. *The Truth About Stories: A Native Narrative.* Minneapolis: University of Minnesota Press, 2005.

Meyers, Thomas P. *Birth and Rebirth of the Omaha.* Lincoln: University of Nebraska Press, 1992.

Olson, Paul, ed. *The Book of the Omaha.* Lincoln: Nebraska Curriculum Development Center, 1979.

Omaha Tribe of Nebraska. "Omaha Tribal Indian Child Welfare." Macy NE: Omaha Tribal Indian Child Welfare Office, 2000.

Ridington, Robin, and Dennis Hastings. *Blessing for a Long Time: The Sacred Pole of the Omaha Tribe.* Lincoln: University of Nebraska Press, 1997.

Silko, Leslie Marmon. *Gardens in the Dunes.* New York: Simon and Schuster, 1999.

Stabler, Eunice W. *How Beautiful the Land of my Forefathers.* Wichita: Wichita Eagle Press, 1943.

Walker, Barbara, ed. *Out of the Ordinary: Folklore and the Supernatural.* Logan: Utah State University Press, 1995.

Welsch, James. *Omaha Tribal Myths and Trickster Tales.* Lincoln: J and L Lee, 1981.

Wishart, David. *The Dispossession of the Nebraska Indians.* Lincoln: University of Nebraska Press, 1994.

Womack, Craig. *Red on Red.* Minneapolis: University of Minnesota Press, 1999.

INDEX